# financial insight

be the author of

*your life story*

**Jodi Carter**

Copyright © 2023 by Jodi Carter.
Published by FIT 114 Inc.

All rights reserved. This book or any portion thereof may not be reproduced or used in any manner whatsoever without the express written permission of the publisher except for the use of brief quotations in a book review.

Publishing Services provided by Paper Raven Books LLC
Printed in the United States of America
First Printing, 2023

Paperback ISBN 979-8-9887579-4-8
Hardback ISBN 979-8-9887579-5-5

# Praise for *Financial Insight*

"In *Financial Insight*, Jodi does the impossible. Through her graceful take on first seeing us as people, she helps us take away that thing that so many of us attach to money: shame. No matter where you are in your current financial journey, Jodi honors that place and becomes a wise and strategic guide through your travels."
—Tyler Merritt, Author of *I Take My Coffee Black* and Creator of *The Tyler Merritt Project*

"Jodi Carter's *Financial Insight* is a must-read for anyone who is looking for a more thoughtful and action-oriented approach to their finances. Working with Jodi completely revolutionized the way I view my own financial journey, helping me to identify and eliminate points of fear in order to take action and actually build wealth. I'm thrilled that readers around the world will now get to reap the benefits of her wisdom too. Don't miss the opportunity to experience what it feels like to be coached by Jodi personally!"
—Macy Schmidt, Music Director and Orchestrator, *Forbes 30 Under 30*

"This book is the answer for all of us who were raised in a time where money was the focus of everything, and yet we were never taught what to actually do with it. Jodi breaks it down so you no longer have to be afraid of money and can make it work for you."
—James Monroe Iglehart, Tony Award-Winning Actor and Director

"Jodi's guidance in explaining how our relationship with money impacts the way it flows in our lives is a godsend! She illuminates money matters in a way that is so inviting and welcoming! Trust me. You need this book in your life!"

—Derrick Baskin, Grammy and Tony Award Nominee

"Jodi's calm, kind, and clear voice cuts through the fear that is always in the background of our minds when it comes to money. This book will help you see the big picture and begin to chart your own course with clarity and confidence. *Financial Insight* is the education we all need and is especially welcoming for those with a nontraditional career like mine. This book is worth its weight in gold!"

—Scott Schofield, Actor, Writer, Producer, and Speaker

"*Financial Insight* is your passport to unlocking financial freedom. This extraordinary book combines expert guidance and practical strategies to empower you to take control, make smarter decisions, and create a brighter future. Authored by the wonderfully captivating Jodi Carter, this must-read book presents transformative insights that resonate with your deeply personal journey towards financial success, allowing you to script your own prosperous life story."

—Ean Castellanos, Actor and Director

# CONTENTS

# INTRODUCTION

It breaks my heart to see how unapproachable the topic of money has become. How did talking about money, which is at the root of everything we do, become a conversation that feels so unsafe? Discussing money is considered taboo in public, except in ways used to judge and shame others. In private, it lives at the core of some of the most challenging conversations we have with spouses, partners, children, siblings, parents, friends, roommates, coworkers, bosses, and employees. Even in settings where it is the main topic, like with a financial advisor, it's uncomfortable.

Money is perceived as mysterious, intimidating, and scary. We are riddled with judgment because we relate to it like a game with winners and losers. We are paralyzed by fear and shame because we believe we are failing or not measuring up to arbitrary standards. In the best of circumstances, when all is going well, we suffer with uncertainty and worry about what we could do better. We know how important money is, but because we don't feel safe discussing it, we pretend it isn't at the heart of every choice we make. We go to great lengths to avoid talking about it.

I use "we" here because this is a phenomenon of the human experience. No one is immune from this. Compounding this problem, if we can't talk about it, where do we learn about it? The secrecy is deafening. Once I understood how pervasive this problem was, it became my mission to create a place where we would regard money not only as a safe topic but a foundational conversation for happiness.

My understanding of money is both professional and personal. I am a Certified Public Accountant (CPA), and I have spent over three decades working with individuals and small business owners. The primary purpose of my business was to help them navigate the complexities of taxes, but that purpose became secondary for me when I saw the epidemic struggle that existed in conversations about money. The decisions that people make, in every area of their lives, are financial decisions. When making a major purchase, such as a car or a home, money is involved. For career choices, money is involved. When advancing a relationship to cohabiting or marriage, money is involved. Thinking of having children? Money is involved. Attending a social event? Money. Deciding whether or not to brush your teeth before bed? Money. If toothpaste isn't compelling enough for you, think of the dental bills! Every choice is a financial choice, but where was *Financial Choices 101* in our education? I was not taught how to make good financial choices in accounting classes either. When I was starting my career as a CPA in my twenties, my awareness about money was informed by both my own circumstances and also the impact of choices in my clients' lives as well.

I was fascinated by the similar threads in every life, no matter how different their circumstances. The amount of money that people earned, or could access, was not the determining factor in the quality of their decision-making. There were those with significant amounts of money flowing through their lives that struggled and others that flourished. Alternatively, some with very few resources flourished, while others struggled. More money was not the answer to financial success. It was in the decision-making that their lives unfolded in ways that they perceived as good or bad. But it wasn't as simple as right and wrong decisions that could be prescribed based on financial information. There was a quality to the decision-making that seemed elusive to me. I was determined to understand what led to success and what led to undesirable outcomes.

My curiosity was on high alert, as I observed my clients, mentors, family, and friends. I felt the same fear and uncertainty in my own life that everyone around me experienced. We all make decisions every day. Those choices determine how our story unfolds, but there is no place to learn how to do this well. What was available to me was a viewpoint that others could not access. I saw the details of so many lives. This gave me a unique perspective and allowed me to experience personal growth in what turned out to be a master class of life lessons from every scenario one could imagine. This is how I discovered the previously elusive quality to decision-making that I call *financial insight.*

I observed individuals who had clarity about what was most important in their lives, and they were not swayed by outside pressure. They were the rare few. Most people didn't have this kind of clarity and, instead, made choices focused on how they were perceived, by themselves as well as others. This emotional component to the decision-making became obvious to me in each conversation with clients. But there was more to it. Those that knew their financial circumstances well enough to talk about monthly spending, savings, earnings, and debt were able to see a clearer picture even before asking for guidance. Those that asked for my opinion without any information available seemed to roll the dice and hope for the best. The level of knowledge of one's finances was evident in an initial brief conversation. As I observed more and more decisions and the outcomes, I discovered that success was achieved when these two key factors existed together. *Financial insight* occurs when you align the understanding of what matters most to you with a solid knowledge of your financial facts.

Throughout this book, I will introduce you to people with whom I have worked. Their stories will help demonstrate how *financial insight* works. You will likely identify with circumstances similar to your own. And you will gain clarity about the inner workings of your relationship with money by learning about non-similar circumstances too. It may be the story that is least like yours that will cause your mindset shift because you won't be caught up in the emotions of it. I invite you to learn from each example. Some of the stories will evoke feelings of sadness, sympathy, or empathy. Others will inspire. The transformations that my clients experienced are extraordinary, and many expressed a desire to share their stories here. I chose common themes in many of our lives, such as determining how much to spend on a home or paying off debt once and for all. Often when I tell a story, someone I worked with has said, "Was that me you were talking about?!" Quite often, the answer is no, but we are all so alike in some ways that we easily see ourselves in the story of another.

One of the most challenging aspects of talking about money is the inevitable judgment. This will show up in a few ways because you really can't help but have an opinion when you look into the lives of others. You will catch yourself judging others, yourself, and me. That is natural, but it also isn't helpful in this endeavor. The purpose of each story is to help you understand yourself better. I invite you to notice the judgment and let it go. When you can do that for others, you learn to more easily do it for yourself. Notice if you have already begun judging whether this book will help or if you won't be able to gain anything from it. You have core beliefs that whisper to you, and sometimes shout, about whether you will ever be successful. You judge yourself on that scale every day. We will work on this as you learn to redefine your personal measures of success with *financial insight.*

There is one story that you might find yourself judging more than others, and that is my own. While I have more than enough stories from others that could fill volumes of books, I will share my story for two reasons. By learning about my journey, you will come to know that I truly understand the learning process from direct experience. I was the first person that I taught how to possess and apply *financial insight.* The second reason is that because talking about money feels vulnerable, I would not ask you to do so without opening up in the same way. As I said earlier, I did not have this education either. I observed and learned while I lived my life. I made plenty of decisions before I understood *financial insight.*

After many years of guiding my tax clients with the concepts of *financial insight,* I made this the focus of my work. Financial Insight

Training (FIT) evolved to a thriving online community called the FIT Universe, which includes a series of courses, live workshops, and private coaching for members. The mission to change the way we collectively talk about money now exists as a place for people to access a new way of thinking, along with the guidance for action steps that transform their lives. With *financial insight*, you gain awareness of the story you are writing with each decision. A paradigm shift occurs.

This book illuminates the collective belief system that we inherited from the past. It demonstrates the flaws in the decision process that keep us from living our best lives. Every choice you make has the potential to change your story. If you are not aware of the optimal way to make decisions, you write your story in a way that will not fully engage your hopes and dreams. When you understand why money became so challenging for all of us, you will be empowered to pursue the direction of the life you desire.

It is my intention for this book to be read as if we are having a conversation. I want you to feel seen and heard and to gain trust that I understand the challenges. Even without knowing your unique circumstances, you will know that I am aware of the feelings you experience. When someone meets with me for the first time, they tell me why they reached out. Take a moment now to think about what you would share with me to help me get to know you. Do you believe that you missed out on learning about money because of your family circumstances? Do you believe that you made mistakes or are starting late? Are you managing well enough but hoping to find guidance to address specific concerns? We all grapple with the lack of education around money simply because there was no place to learn about it. You did your best based on what you knew how to do. I want to make sure you received that statement fully, so I'm going to say it again. I have no doubt that you did your best based on what you knew how to do. It is important that you know that too. It is normal to look back on some choices, wishing for a do-over, but that doesn't negate any past choice. You did your best. Your current circumstances are our starting point, and you are here because you want to learn.

Now, for my favorite moment in every introductory meeting: I welcome you to a conversation about money that is comfortable and empowering. The typical response here is a deep breath, or sigh of relief, with a declaration of, "Wow, I feel better already." I hope you feel that too.

"Do the best you can until you know better.
Then, when you know better, do better."

—Maya Angelou

# Part I

# Your Life Story

CHAPTER 1

# Your Relationship with Money

What are three adjectives that describe your relationship with money?

We begin with this question because it shifts focus to the present moment. I know you want to tell your whole story, and we will get there, I promise. For now, just consider this moment and how you feel about this relationship. I ask this question of every new client and in every workshop. The adjectives shared most often are charged with emotion, and they typically fall into one of four categories: fear, shame, regret, and, in the best of circumstances, uncertainty.

When I speak in a group setting, I share the adjective responses and am met with oohs, ahhs, and chuckles expressing the genuine surprise about how universal these feelings are. This common thread of stress and struggle is troubling, but it opens the door to an important observation. Most people assume that they are the only one having a negative experience with money. The realization that this is a common problem provides some relief. It is not your fault that money is challenging for you. You simply were not taught! There was no education to guide you in the process of decision-making. It was simply the progression of aging that made you an adult and gave you authority over money. Without any instruction, you were expected to manage it well. Even if you had family or mentors who offered their beliefs and strategies, molding your ideas is not education. The beliefs and financial strategies of others may or may not support you in the pursuit of the life to which you aspire.

If this is the first time that you are considering your relationship with money, you are establishing an awareness that did not exist before. Were you aware that it was a relationship? The definition of relationship is "the way in which two or more concepts, objects, or people are connected, or the state of being connected."[1] Money is typically treated as a tool that you obtain and use. This ignores the complexity of how money impacts every part of your life. Recognizing money as a relationship, and one of the most important relationships in your life, is vital. All other parts of your life, including your relationships with other people, will be impacted by the quality of your relationship with money.

As you turn your attention to money in this new way, a shift occurs. In the past, you may have thought of your "financial life" to mean how you handled money. Money cannot be removed from the conversation about your life, and life cannot be removed from your conversation about money. Do you have another life that is not tied to your finances? What elements of your life or daily activities have no connection to money? *Financial* is not an adjective that describes life; it is an essential part of your story. Shifting your focus to your life, without qualification, allows you to see the bigger picture. There is a direct correlation between the quality of your relationship with money and your ability to achieve happiness in your life.

With this perspective, the idea of "financial success" as a goal begins to morph into a distraction from achieving happiness in your life. By focusing on achieving success as a function of money, you are more likely to make mistakes. For example, if you are offered a promotion with a significant increase in pay and ignore how you dislike the company or the demands of the job, you move away from happiness to

1 "relationship, n," Oxford Languages and Google, Oxford University Press, March 2023, web, accessed January 11, 2023.

achieve a financial win. This is not success. Each individual needs to define success for themselves. Only with that understanding can you determine how to move money in the direction of the life experience you desire.

One of our biggest challenges is the mass confusion between the idea of "having it all" and "having all of it." The impact of marketing and media, especially social media, causes a hum of dissatisfaction in the background of our lives. When you take the time to think about what you most want in your life, you will become aware that outside sources often pull you away from what you truly want. Eliminating the noise that comes from comparing yourself to others will allow you to find a path that is truly yours. Rather than comparing yourself to others, define your best life. What are your dreams? Where are you today in relation to those dreams? This will be your guide to establish a roadmap and allow you to use your newfound awareness to achieve your personal definition of success. That is the work ahead, but first, we need to start where you are and tell your story.

Every conversation with a new client begins in a similar way. There is some form of "no one taught me!" followed by an origin story. "My parents didn't do well with money" or "they didn't like to talk about it." For some, it is a story of being sheltered or, for others, one of being taken care of to their own detriment. There are some that believe they should have learned but were irresponsible. Others declare this is finally the time for adulting because circumstances changed in a positive way that will make it a successful endeavor, while others believe they ruined any chance of success and are now desperate for guidance. In each scenario, there is just one real point to be made: this person realized that their relationship with money needs attention.

For many years, I listened to these conversation openers and wondered why each individual has to face this reckoning. What if no one was ever taken by surprise or dismay again? What if we didn't have to experience fear or pain to take on our finances in a meaningful way?

How can we nurture this relationship from early education into adulthood? How might that change the achievement of one's best life to be the standard, rather than the exception? And what would the common understanding of success be if defining success was, in fact, common?

I think of *financial insight* as a discovery. I didn't invent it. It existed in the lives of people I was lucky enough to observe. I was also lucky to observe the lack of it in others. It was the contrast that made me aware of it. During that time of realization, I was no different than anyone who comes to work with me now. I did my best, with nothing other than my origin story and dreams of doing better. I wasn't what you may think of as a typical accountant. It's true that I love numbers, especially when they represent money. But what I really love is the story that money tells. The way people use money has always fascinated me. It is a language, and I am an interpreter. It expresses what one thinks of themselves and others. It shows their inner thoughts. I see their insecurities and fears. I see them express love and joy. I can tell the difference between their wants, needs, obligations, and aspirations. I see them fret over choices, be paralyzed by them, or never consider a consequence. It all reveals their inner story to me. I was in the unique position to watch life stories unfold. The unspoken themes led to their next joy or sorrow. Yet it was all invisible to them. They could not seem to see or hear the story they told through their relationship with money.

I didn't understand this immediately. As I look back now, my own thoughts were based on the common misconception of the haves and have-nots as if it was truth. On the surface, it seemed like there were winners and losers. Then, more and more, I encountered smart, capable people who struggled and others who, seemingly by instinct, excelled. When I realized that more money was not indicative of success and that less money did not prevent success, my curiosity grew. While I tried to understand these observations, I experienced hard lessons in my own life. I made many mistakes and had to find my own way. In retrospect, I can say that I was the first student of FIT!

When you spend time with friends or family and talk about what's happening in your life, you are a narrator. You describe your life as a series of events, concerns, decisions, and goals. Many of us spend as much time talking about our life as we do living it! When you talk about it, you describe it as if it is happening to you. The people that you are close to, and even some acquaintances, receive updates routinely. When you tell your story to someone new, you go back through your history to explain how you reached your current circumstances. You describe your childhood and tell the tale of your parents, their mistakes, and the ways that they did or didn't communicate with you. You talk about how you learned tough lessons. You may recognize that you didn't know better so you couldn't have done better. You remember the missed opportunities, and you bask in the glory of the best outcomes. You describe your home or job as either a dream come true or a stepping stone. You express regret about your current struggles and proclaim victory over perceived successes.

You see your story as an unfolding that includes some wins and some losses. There are choices that you are proud of and others that you perceive as mistakes. It is a retrospective based on the historical events that you deem important. Throughout your storytelling, if you mention money at all, it is incidental to the story. But your story is not your past. It is a work in progress. It began sometime in childhood when you first became aware of money. It continues for as long as you live. You are reading this book somewhere in the middle of your story. I know that to be true because you are still alive! Now, with this awareness, you are no longer the narrator but instead the writer.

Each of the events you describe were, at one point, a "now" in which you made a choice. Every choice in your past determined the next part of the path forward. The story isn't only in the rearview mirror;

it is also the road ahead. The direction you choose with each decision you make determines the next part of your story.

Looking back on those memorable moments gives you an opportunity to consider your thought process at that time. What influenced you? Most importantly, it allows you to own the story you write. With each past choice, regardless of the outcome, you took action. In those actions, you wrote a scene in your story. You may feel like you rushed from one phase to the next or like you just tried to keep up with the speed of life, rather than being in charge of it. And yet you know that you are the one making each decision about what to eat, what to wear, and where to work. Every part of your life is your story. With each choice you make, you express yourself and plan your future.

From your daily coffee to your career, home, and relationship, every choice is a financial choice, but seeing it this way is not the norm. Instead, money is seen as a tool, rather than the deeply personal relationship that determines how you live. The notion that your choices are not about money is the collective pretense of our society. It is considered impolite to talk about money and uncomfortable to bring it up in most conversations, so it feels wrong to make it a primary concern.

When you embrace being the author of your story, knowing that your future is determined by your actions, your approach changes. You think about what works well and the challenges you currently face. You reference past events to help color in the motivations and obstacles that you encountered, but you are more forward-thinking. The difference in mindset that moves you from narrator to author provides a sense of control and power. It will, however, require intention and practice to maintain this way of thinking. As you consider your future plans, you will raise questions and concerns. As quickly as you can recognize that you write the story, you will forget and take the default position that you are not in control. This is an expected challenge with any behavioral changes and the reason why *financial insight* is vital to your success.

James had significant credit card debt and couldn't see how he would ever pay it off. He was afraid that he had done irreversible damage. He was engaged and planning the wedding of their dreams, while fearing his debt would keep him from finding happily ever after. James described the past circumstances that led to the debt. He loved to shop for clothing and home décor. He worked in fashion, and a lavish, beautiful wedding was a priority for him. He believed that if only there was no credit card debt, there would be no problem. This point of view let him off the hook. He focused on the credit card balance and how he wished it didn't exist, rather than acknowledging the habits that caused it. In the weeks following our initial meeting, we worked on a plan to pay off the debt. We addressed the habits that contributed to excessive spending. And yet he continued spending. Each time we spoke, he told the same story that he had dug a hole that was too deep to get out of and declared that nothing would solve this problem.

After a few months of this repeating pattern, I told him that this story was no longer about the past. He was startled by this statement. I pointed out that he was actively digging the hole by continuing to spend in the same way, and this was in his control. I asked, "What is the future story of this debt? The story is not over. It is in this moment that you determine the outcome." With each choice he made since we began working together, he chose more debt. It was time to recognize that this wasn't a circumstance happening *to* him. He was writing the story day by day.

Instead of reviewing the plan and asking if he would pay off his debt, I asked him if he was willing to learn about his relationship with money. He needed to practice making decisions that moved him in the direction of the desired outcome. There were reasons for his spending that went beyond enjoying clothing and home décor. James's belief that he would never pay off his debt informed his choices. If it was true that it would never be paid off, he didn't need to make any effort to do so. Through the recognition that he was the author of his story, he reached a level of clarity he couldn't achieve before. With many years of mounting debt in his past, it was not surprising that the habit change would require time and effort. His willingness to apply what he learned changed the path.

Ready for some good news? As you read this book, your perception will shift. You will see your relationship with money in ways that you have not experienced before. You will look at your past to find valuable lessons. Those lessons will guide your process to create a vision for your future. You will learn about your current circumstances as it relates to the phases that we all experience in our relationship with money. In the past, you may have had glimpses of your potential future life if you were "good with money," but there were gaps in your understanding or skills. Even though you recognized that you are in charge, perhaps you noticed it is difficult to stay in that mindset for long. In your daily actions, your management of obligations, responsibilities, schedules, and relationships all seem to pull you in different directions.

When I look at my calendar, I often think, *Who scheduled all of this?* I feel like someone is trying to do me in! There is so much to do, and there are so many deadlines. I know that I planned it all, and yet it feels like a circumstance I have no control over. That gym appointment was a great idea when I put it in the calendar but not so great when it is time to go. Even the most enjoyable activity feels like a chore. I make plans with friends to eat at my favorite restaurant and see a show that I can't wait to experience. Then, there I am, hours before, wishing I had not planned it and even dreading it. Of course, when I go, I have a great time. I'm so happy and thankful when it is done.

This same phenomenon occurs in your story. You don't know who put this demanding career, partner, or even children in the way of your freedom to do what you want in the moment. Oh, but wait, that was you! You made all of those choices. They all seemed like a good idea when you chose them. Hopefully, upon quiet reflection, you are pleased with those big decisions now, even though there are times that they feel hard. If there are decisions that you truly want to change, the lessons learned will be valuable, and course corrections can be made.

Take a big leap forward in your mind to the version of you that is as old as you can imagine. Think about the story you would like to tell from that point in time. Looking back on a full life, what do you want to highlight? Will you describe the choices that led you to the best of circumstances? Will you share the times that you recognized what wasn't working and took the steps to change course? From that perspective, life is much clearer, but it is also a time when there are fewer choices ahead. Taking control now and owning your status as the author of your story will make for a much better future. If you sit on the sidelines, waiting for somedays and hoping that it will turn out, you squander the opportunity to live the life you want to live. You are in charge. You are in control. You are the author of your story, and the action steps that you take determine the future. Even if the outlook is not ideal *right now*, the future will be determined by what you *write now*.

CHAPTER 2

# Telling Your Story

In 2013, I had an extraordinary opportunity to teach financial literacy at Eximius College Preparatory Academy, a New York City public high school in the Bronx. I created *Decade$*, a program for juniors and seniors, that allowed them to experience the impact of their decisions as their life story unfolded. At each of our five workshops, they aged by a decade.

In our first meeting, I declared it graduation day and assigned them the tasks of choosing a career, researching a starting salary, and determining the cost of their education. All of the students in this community qualified for free undergraduate degrees, but most of them had plans for graduate school and would require financial assistance. In each meeting, personal decisions were made about student loans, careers, marriage, families, and where to live. There was also the sometimes loved and sometimes dreaded "bag of consequences," in which they reached in, blindly, to draw from issues like credit card debt, divorce, bonuses, or an inheritance. I guided them on calculations about their income and expenses. Every step of the way, there was a circumstance and an outcome connected by ten years. At our last meeting, when they reviewed the life they experienced from age twenty to sixty in just five months, their conclusions were filled with the wisdom of old age.

As I listened to their biggest takeaways during our last session, I was astonished by how clearly they learned the lessons. One young woman shared, "I want to have a large family, so I am going to consider living somewhere that a big home isn't quite as expensive." Another said, "Kids are expensive! I'm going to wait a while and make sure that's what I want. I'll save for it, but if I don't do it, I'll travel instead!" A young man whose answer to every challenge was "I'll just eat ramen!" thoughtfully said, "I want to make sure that I choose a spouse who thinks about money the way that I do. We won't fight and can build a great life." I still get tears in my eyes when I remember this moment. The way *Decade$* taught the impact of decision-making was incredibly special. It provided these teenagers with a breakdown of adulthood. It considered not just the big decision points but also the connections between them. It took an exciting, and in many ways daunting, future and allowed them to wonder what was most important to them in each phase.

We are hardwired to tell stories through a framework of beginning, middle, and end. In discussions about money, this commonly sets up a perspective of life in thirds, with childhood, adulthood, and later life. The contrast between this perspective and that which the students in *Decade$* came to understand was very revealing. The years ahead seemed daunting until they experienced the connections between each phase of their lives. Your life is obviously much more complex than a beginning, middle, and end, so it is important to acknowledge how this sweeping view of life in thirds makes it difficult to feel in control of your story. The complexity of your relationship with money makes mentally partitioning your life in thirds an obstacle to your success. Let's examine this point of view to help you dismantle this kind of thinking.

The first third, aka the beginning, is commonly considered the period that carries you from childhood through education. It typically encompasses the first eighteen to twenty-two years of your life. In this part of your story, your family and upbringing are the primary characters and plots. You describe what you witnessed, how you perceived it, and what impact you believe it had on you. In most of this phase, you see yourself as lacking in control. It is a waiting period. You have not yet arrived, but you are learning. As decision-making begins to transfer to you in the latter part of this phase, you are very reliant on others for guidance.

Learning does not end abruptly when your education is complete. Setting aside the fact that your education does not include any valuable information about money, it is not possible to know enough about yourself—your goals, dreams, or desires—to adequately prepare for the rest of your life while between the ages of eighteen and twenty-two. No one has all of the knowledge they need upon emerging from high school or college and beginning full-time employment! The most valuable time for learning, after you complete your education, shouldn't be ignored. The process continues as you find your footing for the next decade or more. Considering the length of our lives, this is not an equal third. You are being ripped off!

After your education is complete and you start your first job, the middle third based on this perspective, aka adulthood, begins. The adulthood phase continues until you stop working. Your career and/or your family is the focus of your story. In this phase, you recognize that you have some control but also grapple with circumstances that seem to interfere. This period is collectively accepted as an excessively long third that can last as many as fifty years.

Looking at your working years as a whole is far too broad of a period. It sets you up for running a race at an unsustainable pace. You feel behind your peers. You wish you were closer to your goals long before they are even possible. A couple searching for their dream home, a decade before they can afford it, spends years unhappy because their focus is unattainable. As this decades-long middle phase of adulthood approaches the later stages, you look back, wishing the lessons you learned had come sooner. You regret the pressure that caused you to accept debt as an option. Instead of acknowledging the inevitable growth that comes with age, you perceive earlier choices as mistakes and blame yourself for perceived failures. Even in the best of circumstances, you wish you could gain some of that time back because you see the trajectory more clearly. Including your twenties and thirties in the same phase as your fifties and sixties makes no sense. And yet all of this is included in the expansive middle third.

The end is what many refer to as retirement. This is the time period when you no longer work or transition to a type of work outside of your original career path. You aspire to these alleged golden years throughout your life. Here, you cross a self-designated finish line that you hope brings you a level of peace and happiness. In this phase, you reflect on what you accomplished and find a level of satisfaction to ride out the remaining years. If you rush to this phase, it could be longer, but for most, it encompasses fifteen to thirty years, depending on your health.

There may come a time that you stop working. This is not true for everyone. More importantly, why must you wait until that time to experience the freedom that you desire? Aging is happening. No matter how you try to avoid it, it will happen. I always loved the way my grandmother described aging, "It's no good getting old, but the alternative is not better!" In the best of circumstances, you will live a long life. In the view of life in thirds, you spend those later years conducting a post-game analysis as you reflect on your life through a binary lens of good/bad, success/failure, or win/loss. These measures don't tell the story with all of the nuance and experience that impacted a full life. This race-to-the-finish mentality distracts you from the stages that you move through as an adult. The most dynamic time of your life is behind you, and you don't realize it until it is in the past.

Each decision you make, whether it is a small part of your daily routine or a significant life event, is part of the writing of your story. Holding onto this thought in the day-to-day of life is not easy! Consider aspects that you work on for a while, such as committing to exercise, eating well, finding a new job, or spending more time with loved ones. You set goals, create plans, and determine action steps. Then, habits take over, or circumstances challenge your plan, and you find yourself feeling disappointed or frustrated. You decide to start over. Perhaps you make a declaration based on a date on the calendar, or you go to bed thinking, *"Tomorrow is the day I..."* And you repeat this process. If you notice a one-step-forward, two-steps-back kind of dance in your behavior, it is because the connection between action and result is difficult to see in the long view. It is especially difficult to focus on this when you don't feel like an author writing a story and, instead, feel like life is happening to you.

We start adulthood in hot pursuit of various goals. We race to what we think we want, measuring our progress, and always feeling behind schedule. This hints at a flaw in our collective approach to the pursuit of future achievements. With the mentality of "eyes on the prize," you race past your actual life. Like sprinting in a marathon, the pace doesn't match the timeline. You only believe you're winning this race if you can see the end working out as planned. If it isn't looking good, you believe that it wasn't your fault! You swear you would have been successful if it wasn't for the lack of guidance from parents, the perfect job that remained out of reach, the ugly divorce, the demands of children, partners, parents, friends, etc. You are convinced that, under no circumstance, *your* actions veered you off course!

As an emerging adult, you are thrust into the middle of the story. There is an expectation that you know what comes next. Here is the flaw—your story is about finding your way. It is about making choices, experiencing consequences, and making new choices. The quality of your decision-making isn't measured by arbitrary results. The only valid measure of success is your happiness. You can be as happy on the way to a goal as when you achieve it. Success is not an endgame or distant point in the future. Saving the down payment for a home is as much of a success as buying the home. Day by day, choice by choice, you tell your story.

Because he grew up in these conversations with me, Scott, my twenty-five-year-old nephew, is keenly aware of this, and yet the idea of an endgame still distracts him. He is doing great already. Just a few years into his career, he has a lot of potential for growth in a company that he likes. He lives in his own apartment, is proudly independent, and learns about his relationship with money in our work together. However, each time we talk, he expresses his frustration with not making more money yet and having to wait to see the future impact of his current decisions. He wonders about the future in a way that leaves him feeling dissatisfied with the present.

While I share openly with clients about my path, Scott is in my life observing it as a witness. He asks many questions about how I make decisions and often comments about his envy of the freedom I have. He is three years into a decades-long journey, but due to cultural pressures, his mindset is forming as stress and struggle. There is no language for him to express his current phase. There is only the finish line that he cannot reach. He even addresses this by saying, "I know that I can't be forty-five when I'm twenty-five, but I want the forty-five-year-old things now!"

To shift his mindset, I reintroduced myself to Scott. At twenty-five, I worked eighty to a hundred hours each week and lived in my parents' home. For the next few years, I spent more than I earned and began my debt journey. It wasn't until I was forty-five that I completed my course correction and began making the kinds of thoughtful decisions that Scott already executes skillfully. My process required years of mistakes because there was no place to learn the decision-making skills. During those years, I was not aware that I was writing a story of struggle. I did my best based on my dysfunctional relationship with money. The journey I took will look nothing like the path Scott is on. What took me twenty years can be accomplished in a much shorter period with the understanding and application of *financial insight*.

Scott is beginning his path on a strong foundation. I'm envious of *him*! If we were contemporaries, he would see that he was far ahead of me in the development of a healthy relationship with money and that the future holds all of his dreams. I frequently remind Scott that he is writing his story today. There is no sprint needed. The measures of happiness exist where he is now and how he sets up the future.

Meandering through life, wondering how it will turn out, is the result of the life-in-thirds perspective. Throughout life, not just at the end, it's important to reflect on the past for lessons learned and to use that information to know yourself better. Thoughtfully considering the future is also important for direction and to use that information to guide your action steps. Now, the present moment, is where you write your story. *Financial insight* allows you to embrace the present moment, in every chapter of your life, and skillfully make decisions that tell your story with intention.

CHAPTER 3

# Adulting

There was a time when becoming an adult was a curated path. The transition from child to teenager to adult was very clear. An adult had a job, a spouse, and a home and began a family. Check the boxes on this simple list, and poof! You are an adult. That path still exists for many, although it is more fraught. Finding the job, spouse, and home is not as simple as it once was. Some who follow this path do so because they believe it is expected of them. They might not participate in the declaration of this dream. They follow the milestones on the list to please their family and friends. Once they check the boxes, they might find they did not consider their own dreams and desires. I call this "doing next syndrome." Many times, I have coached someone who said, "I don't know how I got here" or "If I had thought about it more when I was younger, my life would be very different."

The high divorce rate begs the question: is the decision to get married wrong so often? Before we go too far down that path, let's look at it from the perspective of the end of a marriage. As individuals learn more about themselves over time, they may come to understand that the partner they chose is no longer right for them. Their spouse may have been an appropriate partner based on what they knew about themselves at the time of the choice, but that might not have been enough information. Whether the person moved forward based on a preordained checklist or lack of a deeper understanding about themselves, time would have made a difference.

The same is true of a career. At eighteen, when you finished high school, did you know enough about yourself or the world to choose a career path that you would similarly desire in twenty years or more? This is not a question of whether or not you would be successful. It is a question of how you want to spend your time. If you had a few years to explore different options before pursuing the next level of education, would you have made a different choice?

"Doing next syndrome" is best described as a sense of bewilderment. You look at your life and wonder "what if?" You may have great success in your career, love your spouse and children, and still feel this way. Even acknowledging these kinds of thoughts may cause you to feel uncomfortable. The good news is that there are course corrections that don't require you to burn it all down. Unfortunately, many people in this situation do not know this, and they take steps that cause it all to implode.

When I first heard the word *adulting* from my millennial nephew, Michael, I had mixed feelings. My first reaction was, "That's not a word," and yet I could see that he used it to describe a new concept. I confess that I was a little annoyed! I obviously became an adult without needing it to be a verb. Why didn't I need a word that described the process? Why was this word becoming so popular?

The notion of adulting began when following the checklist was no longer the common path. The expectation of marriage and family as the top priority slowly faded in the 1980s and 1990s, during my Generation X twenties. By the time Michael was in college in the 2010s, those expectations were no longer the norm. The world changed drastically during our twenty-three-year age gap. He schooled me about the challenges from a whole new perspective, and I understood why a new word was needed to describe this struggle.

Adulting focuses on independence. The path you choose for your career, relationship, and home centers around your ability to achieve independence. Even in finding relationships, independence has become a marker of being ready for partnering. The ability to support yourself and live outside of your family home has become the new measure of being an adult.

I don't recall my grandparents talking about the years that they lived with roommates! They went from their parents' home to living with their spouse. Millennials, and now Generation Z-ers, seek coaching with me to determine when they can move from roommates to a place of their own. That's two steps before cohabitation with a partner. Many of the millennials are in their thirties and forties at this stage, and they have had more time to learn about themselves. While prior generations might see this as a delay, it is instead a benefit that gives them more clarity in the choices they make.

With independence leading the way, the impact of family support becomes a factor. For those encouraged and guided by family, it may appear that they have an advantage, but often, this family support is a hindrance to achieving independence. When the prior generation attempts to be helpful, the individual's process is disrupted.

In my work with the Grant family, I had a very difficult conversation with Jon, the father of Jeff and Lauren, who were both in their thirties. Jon and his wife, Anne, were very frustrated with the choices their children were making. Jon shared, "We helped each of them buy homes by giving them a down payment. They both work but are not making enough money to make the mortgage payments, so we are still helping." When I asked how they decided on the amount to spend on the homes for their children, he said, "We wanted them to have nice places to live." Not surprisingly, he was quite offended when I told him that he was a barrier to the success of his children. I asked him what he and Anne were doing at that age.

He became momentarily disoriented by the comparison and then proudly declared, "We were married with two children and living in a home that we bought on our own." He went on to explain that they were fortunate to have parents who helped with a down payment but only after they showed themselves to be worthy and demonstrated the ability to pay their monthly bills. He said, "We did not quit jobs that we didn't like, and we did not change our minds about our career paths, multiple times, like our kids have." I gently suggested that his frustration occurred because he blamed his kids for wanting to find a path that made them happy. The purchases of the homes were not decisions that Jeff or Lauren made, but he expected them to take responsibility for those choices. I asked him how his kids were supposed to find their way if they were "helped into submission." For Jeff and Lauren, learning was delayed by more than ten years because of the parental interference. Even in their forties, Jon was cc'd on every email with their CPA! Jeff and Lauren struggled to feel independent because Jon kept solving their problems with more money.

For those of us who struggled to make it on our own, that sounds like a wonderful problem to have. Notice that, in either case, the struggle is still there. Any barrier to independence has the same impact on personal growth. Jon's notion of setting up his children for success actually impeded their independence. His desire to help could have been a true boost for them, instead of a perpetuation of the problem. After paying for their education, he could have offered them a year to explore their career choice. He could have worked with them to teach the habits he adopted for saving and paying bills. He could have told them he would match what they saved to help them live on their own. He could have gotten out of the way completely and waited to see how they did. It was ten years after our initial uncomfortable conversation when Jon told me, "Both of my kids are willing to take on the responsibilities. I need to stop interfering." I asked him if that echoed my suggestion from a decade before and frequently over the years. We finally shared a laugh about this saga.

The word *adulting* is often used in a negative connotation to describe a difficulty. I have come to see it as an opportunity to address the desire for independence and an opening for the conversations needed to build a strong foundation for decision-making. To achieve independence, you first need to understand what matters most to you. Taking the time to discover who you are as an adult should not be rushed. Handled with a sense of ease, this can be exciting, rather than stressful.

Instead of racing to a finish line, you can take your time checking out the scenery! What kind of work calls to you? Where do you want to live? What kind of partner will enhance your life? And while you learn about yourself, you will learn about your relationship with money. The world of finance does not have to be complicated, and you can learn how to handle money in the ways that bring you the most happiness. There are no cookie-cutter formulas to follow. Whatever age you are in this moment, whatever the circumstances, you will begin right here. This is where you are in your story. It is the next step that matters, and then the next after that. With *financial insight,* you will naturally excel at the skills needed to move money in the direction of your best life.

CHAPTER 4

# Transitions and Decision-Making Skills

Life is filled with transitions that require us to make decisions. In previous generations, the primary decisions of work, home, and relationship were made, and it was rare for them to be changed. According to a 2019 survey by the Bureau of Labor Statistics, the average number of jobs in a lifetime for baby boomers is twelve.[2] That number is expected to be much higher for Generation X, millennials, and future generations. Staying in one home for decades is unheard of now. Have you ever been to, or even heard of, a "mortgage-burning party?" Folks used to pay off their homes after thirty years and celebrate by burning the loan documents. They continued to live there with no more payments. While the divorce rate has decreased in recent years, it is still estimated to be 40 percent of first marriages.[3] In the current era, it is unlikely that you will have one job, one home, or even one partner.

With the likelihood of many transitions in your life, the skill of decision-making is vital. These broad areas of work, home, and relationship don't account for the many choices one makes about health, spirituality, family, friends, and leisure. Feeling overwhelmed

2 Alison Doyle, "How Often Do People Change Jobs?," The Balance, June 15, 2020, https://www.thebalancemoney.com/how-often-do-people-change-jobs-2060467.

3 Belinda Luscombe, "The Divorce Rate Is Dropping," Time, November 26, 2018, https://time.com/5434949/divorce-rate-children-marriage-benefits/.

already? Even writing this, I'm a little breathless! This may bring to mind choices you made in the past, some with great outcomes and others that could use a do-over. I like to think of the memories that come up quickly as the glaring lights in the rearview mirror. You want to adjust your position to avoid the glare, but they are there, behind you, with important lessons to learn. At the same time, you want to keep your eyes on the road ahead. The decisions that you know are coming soon, and the unforeseen ones, may seem daunting. How will you know if you have made the best choice?

All of these life events have one aspect in common: financial choices. If you are good at making financial choices, it won't matter what circumstances come your way! That exclamation mark indicates an exciting idea, but there is a pretty good chance that this did not make you feel better. Do you feel prepared to make a significant financial decision? Do you have all of the information you need readily available? Do you know what information you need? If your answer to these questions is "I don't know, maybe, I'm not sure," you are not alone.

A typical request for my help begins with a description of a concern. It might be about a decision relating to changing careers, moving, or buying a home. It might be a circumstance like a divorce or an inheritance. All of these are transitions that the individual wants help navigating. After they provide details about the transition, they ask what I think they should do. This is my big moment because I get to tell them that what I think doesn't matter!

In my position, I could spend all day telling people what choice I think they should make based solely on the financial facts. As a matter of fact, there are many so-called financial gurus who do just that. That's ridiculous. No two people with the same amount of money will live the same exact lives. Being prescriptive is the most inappropriate course of action for a financial coach.

Instead, the goal is for you to use *financial insight* to make decisions that move you in the direction of your best life. The skill of aligning your financial feelings and financial facts is what you need to learn and practice. Most of us are better at one side of this than the other. Folks that love data may not want to talk about emotions. Others want to spend all of their energy talking through the emotions and may not feel comfortable with the data. Creating a balance between these two key factors and learning to make decisions with both in mind is how you achieve *financial insight* and the outcomes you most desire.

Setting yourself up for success requires the establishment of a financial environment that supports you. At all times, you are either reactive or proactive. You are reactive if you are not prepared to respond to new circumstances. You are proactive if you have the vital information that you need, even if that means consulting a professional for guidance. Being prepared includes a solid understanding of your finances and a heightened awareness about what matters most to you.

When Nicholas found out that his lease would not be renewed, he was disappointed about leaving a home he had grown to love, but he wasn't worried. He had been working with me for a few years and created a financial environment that gave him great confidence. He sent me a quick note that he wanted to chat about his move and that he was ready with all of the needed information. When we talked, he began by reminding me of his values. These core beliefs that mattered most to him were defined in his work in FIT.

The focus of our conversation was to determine how much he wanted to spend on rent. He shared relevant data points with me because he had set up a system that always provided him with quality information. "I recently paid off all of my debt. I had not planned on the move, but since it is happening, I am considering increasing the amount that I spend on rent with this 'extra' money." Before the landlord made the decision that prompted this move, Nicholas had not considered spending more on his home. He wondered instead about where else he could direct the money, such as a dream vacation or additional savings toward his future. Our conversation turned to his values and what he would want in a new home if he spent more each month.

As we spoke, I couldn't help but think back to the meetings we had when we first started working together. The last time we talked about a new apartment, Nicholas was going through a breakup. He had debt and was afraid to spend too much on an apartment. He was stressed about the moving costs, the security deposit, and so many other factors about living in a new place. That conversation was filled with anxiety and fear. At that time, we hurriedly worked to make a decision, and I told him this was the last time he would find himself feeling pressured and uncertain in this type of circumstance. After that move, we spent time setting up his financial environment.

The conversations that we had brought him much more clarity about what mattered most to him. His values now led every decision. He found a system for reviewing his spending that worked well for him. We established a plan to pay off his debt, and he accumulated savings at the same time. Now, just a few years later, it was a different kind of breakup! The landlord's decision not to offer a renewal of his lease was the catalyst, but the process was proactive and fun.

Nicholas chose a range for the rent for the new apartment. He then made a list of his priorities for the top and bottom of the range. With each apartment that he visited, he was able to decide with ease whether the rent was appropriate for what mattered most to him. There was one space that was at the top of his range that didn't have all of the amenities he wanted for that price. The timeline was growing short, and he found himself feeling pressure to sign any lease.

I shared another one of my grandmother's favorite lines: "Why is what I'm looking for always in the last place I look?"

"Well, when you find it, you stop looking!" I always replied. I encouraged Nicholas to avoid settling because of time pressure and, instead, trust the knowledge that *financial insight* provided him. He continued his search, and the next place he found matched his list and fell in the middle of his price range. He happily signed the lease on his new home, knowing that he made the best choice.

If you don't acknowledge that the transitions in your life require good decision-making skills, and you don't take a proactive approach to prepare with a supportive financial environment, you are more likely to make mistakes. *Financial insight* is a deep, intuitive understanding of your values and an accurate knowledge of your data. With *financial insight*, you are consistently a good decision-maker. Learning and practicing these skills will benefit you more than any advice you could ever seek.

After more than three years of staying close to home because of the global pandemic, Mark and Chris decided it was time for a trip. Many of their friends began traveling, and they were ready too. The past few years had been difficult in their careers because they both worked in industries that were shut down and slow to reopen. They made their way through, and now it was time to celebrate, so they planned a trip to Europe.

They started working with me prior to their trip. We had some great conversations about their money mindsets, but we had not yet reviewed any data. They displayed a lot of resistance and were slow to take action. It wasn't until they returned from their vacation that we met to look at the financial facts. The challenges of the past few years caused them to increase credit card debt. As we worked on a plan for paying off the debt, I asked if they could stop using the cards while they paid them down. This is a key factor to ending the debt cycle. They responded, "Yes, now that the vacation is over, we won't need to use the cards." As we planned the monthly payments and looked at the timeline to pay the balances, I asked how much of the total debt was from their trip. They spent $7,000 on the vacation, and it was all included in the total debt of $20,000. I asked for their indulgence while I showed them a comparison of the debt with and without the vacation included.

They would need four years to pay off the current debt. In comparison, if they had not paid for the trip with their credit cards, they would have only needed two years, and the interest cost would be far less. I knew this was a tough conversation, but the lesson was too valuable to lose. Had we planned ahead, they would have had a clear choice to make. Option #1: postpone the trip until they saved the funds to pay for it, while paying down their debt. Option #2: take the trip and understand that the cost would double the amount spent because of the cost of financing it with credit cards. Asking it another way, I said, "Would the $7,000 trip be worth $14,000 if it meant that you could do it now?"

When I ask this type of question before someone makes a choice, I sit in curiosity! What will they decide? No two clients answer such a question the same way. The combination of financial feelings and financial facts is deeply personal. There is no right answer. The answer you are thinking of right now is yours and yours alone. Only your relationship to the circumstances matters. The most difficult element in this situation was that they made the decision without knowledge of the outcome in advance. The financial environment did not support them in making a confident choice.

Keeping in mind that each individual has a unique relationship with money, I waited for their responses with some concern. I delivered what might be perceived as bad news, but it was my responsibility to make this a teachable moment. Whether they were satisfied or unhappy with the outcome was only part one of the lesson here. The second, and more important part, was learning about the impact of making decisions without *financial insight.*

Their reactions added a third lesson too. This couple was not communicating about money in a way that made either of them comfortable. Mark shared that he was okay with the trip costing more and wouldn't trade the experience or timing for any amount. But he also admitted that he was stressed about money throughout the trip.

He wasn't tallying what they spent and was afraid that they made the situation harder for themselves when they returned home. He recognized that he would have enjoyed himself more if he knew the cost and time to pay it off, instead of packing the weight of uncertainty in his luggage.

Chris was upset about the cost and said he would have preferred to wait a year or two to travel with less cost. He wasn't stressed during the trip and kept spending because he chose to ignore the consequences. He thought they would never get out of debt and saw this trip as a last hurrah before giving up travel for the foreseeable future. Neither of these responses described the dream trip that they wanted. This was a very emotional conversation, and you might be experiencing a very strong temptation to judge here. Notice your reaction and keep in mind that we all have circumstances that can derail us. This is a great opportunity to practice shifting focus to the lessons available.

Setting yourself up for the key elements of a supportive financial environment will also remove the *shoulds* that complicate your decisions. Mark and Chris believed that they should take a vacation because of the timing and because their friends were traveling. Those *shoulds* influenced their choices without any consideration for their values or data. With a focus on the financial feelings and financial facts, they may have taken the same trip, at the same time and cost, but they would have done so without the stress, both during and afterward. After we established a plan to pay off the debt, we reviewed their spending and began working on other adjustments that would allow them to save for their next trip. This pivotal lesson opened up conversations of mindfulness and made *financial insight* the focus of all future decisions.

CHAPTER 5

# The End of Stress and Struggle

To explain my story, first, I need to introduce you to one of my mentors, Robert. He was also an accountant, and I learned so much from him. I learned how to care for clients, how to ask questions to obtain the details we needed, and how to translate our work into information they could easily understand. I watched him help clients make decisions. I sought his advice on every choice I made too. I was vaguely aware that Robert struggled with money himself. It took years for him to open up and share with me that he was deep in debt. His family was spending twice what he was earning. He felt that he never did enough to make them happy, and the relationships, especially with his wife, were strained.

The first time that values and data appeared to me as misaligned, with perfect clarity, was in a conversation with Robert's son. He was five years younger than me and in his early twenties at this time. He said, "My dad has given me so much, but he has never been there for me." Robert wanted to be a good father and husband and believed that doing so meant that he should give his family everything they wanted. Unfortunately, that translated to every "thing." He did not recognize that his time with them would be valued. He worked and worked to earn more so that he could pay for more. The more he worked, the less time he spent with the family. They resented his work, and they spent more and more money to make up for the loss and hurt. When his son made that statement to me, many arguments I overheard between Robert and his wife raced through my mind. This was the subject of all of their fights.

By the time I learned this, I was also living beyond my means. Robert encouraged me to use credit cards for everything I wanted. His philosophy was, "have what you want now and figure out how to pay for it later." I had clearly made a mistake in relying on this person as my mentor, and I needed to figure out how to course correct. First, I had to answer one question to truly help myself. Why did this man who knew so much about money make every choice to his own detriment?

If Robert understood his own values, he wouldn't have struggled as he did. He wouldn't try to solve every problem with more money. He would see the pressure that debt added to his circumstances. He would have the opportunity to define success for himself and make the decisions that resulted in that desired outcome.

Many years later, Robert asked me about the inspiration for the coaching I did with clients. He was a grandfather by this time and still looking for work, still not having time for family because he had never gotten out of debt.

We spoke openly about the difficulties that he faced, and he often apologized to me. "I'm sorry for the bad advice I gave you when you were just getting started." He knew I turned my situation around and asked what inspired me to guide others.

I decided to share the lesson that I learned from his family with an example. I will never forget the sad look on his face when I said, "Your kids didn't want the fancy cars you bought for them. They wanted you to spend time teaching them how to drive." Robert understood how it went wrong but not until it was too late. My inspiration for *financial insight* began with his example of working so hard without defining success for himself. If I could disrupt that path for others, he agreed, it would pay the lesson forward in many ways.

When people begin working with me, they often share a belief that they don't have access to a secret world of information. Money is perceived as a mystery, and they believe that there is some inside scoop to uncover. Sometimes they think they are unfairly denied the information, while they seek relief from a self-diagnosed problem. Others are so fixated on having more money that they become magic seekers—those who search for the quick fix, the big win, and the keys that unlock some hidden door. When I listen to people in this mindset, I notice that their quest is undefined, but they are convinced that more money will resolve any issue. In these pursuits, they describe a stressful relationship with money and fear about the future. They are aware that there is much to learn, and they don't know where to start.

We can end the myths of money as a secret or a mystery right now. A secret is defined as "something that is kept or meant to be kept unknown or unseen by others."[4] With a heightened awareness of your relationship with money, there is nothing unknown. Mystery is defined as "something that is difficult or impossible to understand or explain."[5] The concepts of *financial insight* eliminate any difficulty in understanding money.

Success is dependent on behavior. There are as many people who fail with large sums of money as there are those who succeed with modest amounts. The difference is always in the behavior. I will remind you again and again: no two people with the same amount of money make the same exact choices. The behavior is made up of two key elements. With these two elements aligned, the individual achieves the *financial insight* to consistently make choices that give them ongoing success.

*Financial insight* = Values + Data

4 "secret, n," Oxford Languages and Google, Oxford University Press, March 2023, web, accessed January 11, 2023.

5 "mystery, n," Oxford Languages and Google, Oxford University Press, March 2023, web, accessed January 11, 2023.

Values are what matters most to you. You need clarity about your values, and then you can elevate them to an intuitive knowing. Data is the accurate understanding of your financial facts. When you align these two elements, you make choices based on your personal financial truth. The simplicity of this is sometimes jarring, sometimes disappointing, and, soon after the first experience of it, a huge relief.

The financial industry, including many books, guides, and advisors, take an outside-in approach. You tell them what you have, and they tell you what to do. Even when goals are taken into account, they offer a formula for winning a game about money, rather than life. The rules of the game are to earn and save as much as you can. These rules might be okay if your idea of winning is to die with the most money you can get. What about thriving in your life? The person who works so much that they have no time for the people they love or activities they enjoy is not successful, no matter how much money they earn. Their big home or ample bank account may check boxes in an imagined win column, but they are not thriving. Missing out on life in pursuit of money has dire consequences.

I have seen this play out in so many sad ways. Consider the loving couple who work and sacrifice all for retirement, and when they reach that age, one of them receives a terminal diagnosis. The opposite is not better. Consider someone who lives only for today, with no plans for the future, and then spends years stressed and pressured just trying to survive. These scenarios occur because of a lack of awareness. Living your best life requires mindfulness and practical planning.

Rather than trying to gather tips, take the time to clearly define your vision of a successful life. Be sure that it includes every chapter, not just the end. Keep in mind that your vision is not fixed and unchangeable. As you learn more about yourself over the years, you may add new plans, and remove others from your vision. The experience of life is determined by your choices. Your choices are all influenced by and in service of your finances. Forget the notion of tricks or schemes to achieve success. The information that you need is already available to you. Your plan will be unique. Stress and struggle don't have to be factors, so let that mindset go as you imagine your best life. With your vision for the future in mind, you will be able to gain a new understanding of your story and how *financial insight* supports you in confidently writing the next chapter.

# Part II

# The Chapters in Your Story

CHAPTER 6

# A New View

One of the most frequent statements that people approach me with is, "I don't know how to make financial decisions." Let's challenge that thought. As previously established, every choice is a financial choice. You make choices all day, every day. Some are routine, like your morning coffee or grocery shopping, and others are more significant, like buying a car or a home. You make decisions all the time. It is simply not true that you don't know how. It is more likely that you are not aware of your process. In your life, just like in every life, some decisions led to positive outcomes while others led you to wish you could trade for a do-over. What is missing is the powerful tool of decision-making with *financial insight.*

Imagine if the ability to consistently make choices that moved you in the direction of your best life was a foundational part of your education. Consider the confidence you would have gained by this time. Instead, you may find yourself chasing tips, tools, or opportunities to solve perceived problems. You may even be trying to find solutions without clarity about the questions you are trying to answer. Rather than looking outward, shift your view to your relationship with money, your understanding of what matters most to you, the current circumstances of your financial facts, and your personal definition of success. This refocus is the work of *financial insight.* And yes, it is work.

We collectively fail to connect the decisions that we make with the challenges that we face, especially in the way that money tells our story. We need a new view that keeps you focused on decisions as the pivot points of the life story you are writing. Maintaining awareness that you are the author of your story will lead you to the mindset and behavioral changes that you seek to achieve your goals and dreams. Your challenges and triumphs are not highlights to be recounted at parties. Shifting your attention to the story you tell puts you in an empowering position. Each decision that you make matters. The old view of a life in thirds did not allow you to understand where you are in your story. There are a series of phases that you move through during your life. You can think of them as the chapters in your story.

This concept of chapters is new only in that you were unaware of it. It has always been there. With money treated as a tool and not recognized as the core of every choice, it was not visible to you. As you see it now for the first time, you will be able to reframe your past and find the chapter that resonates with your current circumstances. As this becomes clear, keep reminding yourself that the goal is not to race to the end. It is to be where you are and to learn to make the best decisions accordingly. It will also guide you to the next chapter at a pace that you desire.

We will start with an overview and then examine each phase in more detail. As you read the brief descriptions that follow, I invite you to take the role of an observer. It is always easier to learn when your feelings are not in the mix. For example, consider a time when a friend shared about their relationship troubles. You could immediately see that this partner was not right for them, but it took your friend months (or years!) to break it off. Or perhaps you were the friend that couldn't see it while everyone around you could?! Let my story be an opportunity for clarity about this new view before you work on your story.

The first chapter is *discovery,* and it begins with the very first interaction with money. A child becomes aware of money through the interactions of the adults around them. They hear conversations or witness transactions by simply visiting a store. In our world today, it may be quite mysterious for some kids because they see an item on a phone or tablet, and the next day, it arrives in a box on their doorstep. It will be interesting to see if this next generation has a much later *discovery* period, but I digress!

After the initial impression is formed, awareness grows. The child may become inquisitive, or they may interpret it as magic. Their understanding of the use of money is sculpted by the adults in their life. During the elementary school years, they may be given money for various purposes. They may have some decision-making powers around school lunches or how to use an allowance or gifts. Again, the adults lead by example and share their points of view, and the child learns lessons that they will carry throughout their lives. By the teen years, they have their first experience of earning money. This increases their authority to make decisions.

Then, without any training in financial decision-making, they are thrust into one of the biggest decisions that they make in their life. What is their next step after graduating high school? A seventeen-year-old, with minimal guidance, is asked to choose a path that impacts the rest of their life. Whether they immediately secure a job or continue their education for a chosen career, this is a foundation on which their entire future will rest. The cost of college may or may not be part of the conversation as they choose a school. For many millennials, there was no understanding of the effect that student loans would have on all future decisions. Considering all you know about money in your life as an adult, it suddenly becomes obvious that we ask far too much of our youth.

Just a few years later, we ask them again, in their early twenties, to choose a first job and a place to live and encourage them to begin serious relationships. Through the lens of money, it all seems too soon. Redefining this phase as *discovery* allows us to change our conversations with emerging adults and expands the timeframe to include years well beyond the end of their school days.

*Discovery* continues as they find their way in their twenties, and, for some, this continues longer into their thirties and beyond. As life experiences continue, an *exploration* begins as they learn about themselves as an adult. They have *freedom* to make choices on their own behalf. They ache for more and feel pressured to achieve goals rapidly, even though time is needed.

In my earliest memories, I perceived money to be very important. From the secretive way that my grandfather gave me a dollar each time he visited to the precious way my father handed my mother his paycheck to be promptly taken to the bank, my reverence for money was formed. By age ten, I naturally compared myself to my peers and did not like what I observed. I didn't wear the brand-name jeans or play the latest video games, and I wanted to know why. When I complained to my parents, they were clear about their choices and stood by them. They proudly declared, "All of your friends have working moms, and you have a stay-at-home mom." I was expected to appreciate having my mother at home, even though it meant that we had less money than other families. They believed this was the best decision, and there was no room for debate.

Throughout my adolescence, I perceived this as an awful circumstance and believed that my life was being derailed by my parents' decision. (Oh, the drama!) It was out of my control because my parents were unwilling to consult me on this choice that impacted my life. Having a roof over my head and food in my belly did not register as "care" in my young mind. It wasn't long before I decided that I would always work to pay for what I wanted. I couldn't change my current circumstances, but I planned to live a very different lifestyle when I was a grownup.

After a few part-time retail jobs in my teens, I began working in my intended field at a small accounting firm. The owner drove expensive cars, wore flashy jewelry, and owned multiple homes. Throughout college, I worked full time, while attending school full time, and planned my future. I wanted nice things, and I was determined to earn them. I moved on to another accounting firm after graduating. In making this decision, I had to choose between a higher salary in a larger firm or another small company with lower pay. My goal was to establish my own firm as soon as possible, and the small company gave me the opportunity for faster growth. I was willing to have less money in the short term to assume control sooner.

While I made a thoughtful decision about which job would help me achieve my goal, my day-to-day decisions revealed that my relationship with money was quite dysfunctional! I wanted things, and I wanted them fast. This was why I was susceptible to the bad advice from my mentor, Robert. For the first five years of my career, I spent far more than I earned each year. My credit card debt grew, and I didn't understand the burden that I was creating. Other than having control, I didn't know what I really wanted in most areas of my life. A relationship? A family? A home?

My career was the one aspect that was working well. I had many friends by proximity, rather than ones that shared my interests. I bought a home at twenty-seven and married at thirty-two. These choices were far more about checking boxes than they were about my happiness. The marriage was brief, and by thirty-five, I was in therapy, wondering how I got to this place. I owned my business, but I was deep in debt and even deeper in unhappiness. It was time to explore who I was and what I truly wanted. What would my life look like if I felt freedom?

The *growth* chapter often begins with discomfort. Sometimes this demonstrates itself in the form of a mistake that requires course correction. The individual finds themselves in a challenging circumstance, such as accruing debt or searching for a place to live after a breakup. Or the discomfort may be more subtle—they think about money itself and notice they have been "adulting" for a while, yet still feel like they don't know what they are doing. In other cases, it may be a success, like a windfall with a new salary or bonus that launches *growth*. Most stumble from *discovery* to *growth* with a life event as a catalyst. They aren't aware of the transition but feel fear, shame, regret, or, even in the best of circumstances, uncertainty. They begin seeking resources in the form of advice from others, podcasts, books, or courses. Sadly, until now, there wasn't an explanation of what they needed or even why they were seeking it.

Throughout *growth*, the individual uses the clarity about themselves and the impact of their choices gained through their past experiences. After many life events that required decision-making skills that they were not taught, they are ready to course correct but are unsure how to do so. They seek the satisfaction of *harmony* and *independence* while they attempt to manage a career, family, and their underlying happiness. They spend their energy finding the best path forward. But to what end?

For many, they race to an undefined finish line. They try to win without understanding what winning means. They may have one area that works well so they put all of their energy there and then suffer about what they don't have. Balance becomes more elusive, and they are tired. For nearly half, marriages fall apart. For some, career aspirations are now chores. The choices they made in home, family, and career cause them to spend all that they earn, and they can't make a change, even though they may want to. In the best of circumstances, they check boxes and bide their time until they reach the traditional retirement.

The underlying work of *growth* appears in every life. Whether you seek it or it finds you through difficult circumstances, the opportunity will arise for you to define your life from the point of view of the adult you become. The freedom to live your best life is the not-so-small reward at stake. As I explored my post-divorce, business-owner life, I had work to do in many areas. I wasn't properly caring for my health,

I worked an extraordinary number of hours, and I was headed down a path of more of the same. The course correction required to change the trajectory seemed impossible. That is, until I figured out, quite literally, where I wanted to go. The life that inspired me included being near the culture that I loved to experience, like theater, art, and the energy of the city. Once I realized that I wanted to move to New York City, I was able to see my life with a clarity that I did not have before. Suburban life is lovely if you want to be there, but it was not the right life for me. The desire to make this change became the filter for every choice I made. I needed to pay off my credit card debt, accumulate money for a move, and make sure that my business would thrive in the new location.

After talking about this desire to move for quite a while, I wasn't making any real progress. I was stuck in the transition until a friend boldly asked me, "*When* are you moving?" Habits needed to adjust, and I had to be realistic. I didn't have an answer. He persisted, "Are you just going to keep talking about it, or are you doing it?" I often look back on that conversation with a sense of awe. I remember how jarring it was because, even with the inspiration and clarity I gained, I was stuck and not moving forward.

*Growth* requires the vision to pull you forward, decision-making skills, and the tools to course correct. One of those tools is the relationship between time and money. My friend asking for a "when" launched a plan. To answer his question, I had to map out the course correction in time. I gave myself seven years. The funny part about *growth* is that, once you truly engage, it propels you forward. I completed my seven-year plan in two years! I moved to New York City and began experiencing a life that matched my dreams.

*Joy* is a chapter that is available much sooner than most realize. Previous generations designated the golden years as retirement and grandchildren. They saw it as a time when their responsibilities were completed, and they could live out their lives based on what they accomplished. That might or might not have been a period of *joy*. *Joy* is achieved when you have the power to choose what makes you happy. If you love your work, you don't need to stop working to reach this chapter. If you make thoughtful choices throughout your life, you can achieve *joy* long before those supposed golden years.

The transition from *growth* to *joy* requires a sense of *harmony* and *independence*. Our lives are complex. Many forces pull us in opposing directions. Once you find clarity about your values, what matters most to you, the next step is to work toward harmony in every area of your life. During *growth*, you understand yourself and your desires more than you ever could in your younger days. You also might realize that the choices you made when you were younger seem to prevent you from the course corrections needed. There may be difficult conversations ahead, and you may need to make bold changes or work on long-held beliefs to move yourself forward. The ability to make changes in your best interest, without hesitation and without causing harm to yourself or others, is the *independence* that used to be available only in old age. With proper planning, this is accessible much sooner.

Once I moved to New York City, the world seemed to open its arms. The first year was a little scary from a financial standpoint. I sold my previous home, and, having used up the equity by overspending for two decades, I had no gain to show for it. My routine spending was higher in my new home, and I held my breath to see if my plan for business growth would work.

Even so, I was happy every day. On more than a few occasions, I randomly called my bold friend who pressed for a date for my move and exclaimed, "I'm looking out my window! Can you believe I live here?!" While enjoying the activities that inspired me, I met new friends that shared my interests. I focused on my health, and my business began to grow exponentially. The *harmony* expanded day by day. I began to notice that I made decisions with a level of confidence that I never had before. What was this strange feeling? Ah, *independence!*

My decisions were about living my best life. I determined how much I worked, where I went, and how I spent my time. I used money mindfully to have what I truly needed and wanted. I created FIT because I wanted to do the work that inspired me and help others in a way that felt most meaningful.

The experience of *joy* came in moments when I worked, moments when I played, and moments when I relaxed. It became my measure of success. I am in no way done with my working life, but I achieved *joy*. It exists in my daily experiences and in the path that I plan for the future. After many years of staying close to home, I began to travel again. It was in those trips that I realized that *joy* is far more expansive because there are more choices to be made and more experiences that I want to have. Wait. What? *Joy* is not the finish line? I want more?

Once *joy* is attained, a curiosity emerges. There is more life ahead. Having achieved *joy*, your perspective changes yet again, and it returns you to *discovery*. Experiencing the cyclical nature of the pattern made it clear to me that this was the missing link. Redefining life in thirds to the true phases that we experience led me to the realization that we can cycle through these chapters, at our own pace, and repeat them to achieve more throughout our lives.

This understanding enabled me to see when someone was stuck in *discovery* or *growth*. A decision, or a series of choices, impacted their progress or the lack thereof. In coaching, I ask questions to open ways of thinking that never occurred to them. Heightening awareness about what you experience allows you to reflect on lessons from the past, feel confident in the present, and plan for the future.

In goal setting, an emphasis is often placed on "why" to make sure that you are clear about your reasons for change. This is followed by planning action steps to determine "how" you achieve the goal. Understanding "what" you are working on is as important. When you begin a fitness plan, you identify your reasons for this pursuit, and you plan your nutrition and exercise to fulfill the goal. You may not know all of the details about burning calories or building muscle, but there is a whole industry with this knowledge if you want to learn more. The way that the body works is a known factor. Conversely, when you seek help with your finances, your why and action steps are not supported by an understanding of the inner workings of your life. The feeble attempt made by supposed financial gurus and advisors who say "earn more, spend less" does not even approximate the complexity of the decisions you make throughout your life. There is no one-size-fits-all advice that will suit everyone.

The reason that stress and struggle are the norm is that the progression of your life is undefined. Adulthood, encompassing decades, is far too broad. No two lives will be lived the same way, but the ambiguous instructions in the unwritten user manual for life simply say, "Be an adult." *Financial insight* is deeply personal, and your timeline will be completely unique. You are already writing your story with each decision you make. It is not enough to say you will leave stress and struggle behind. It is the knowledge about the process that will replace stress and struggle with ease and confidence. Expanding your knowledge to understand all of the phases—*discovery, exploration, freedom, growth, harmony, independence,* and *joy*—will empower you to write your story with intention.

CHAPTER 7

# Discovery

There is no greater place to learn about yourself than from your own decisions and experiences. The opportunity to connect the dots and redirect the way forward begins with your chapter of *discovery*. Keeping in mind that you have a relationship with money, let's consider how relationships typically develop. When you meet someone new, you observe them, you notice how you feel around them, and you become curious about future interactions. If they don't treat you well or you don't feel comfortable, hopefully, you choose not to see them again. We don't have that luxury of choice with money. Even if the introduction doesn't go well, we continue in this relationship for the rest of our lives! The early interactions you have with money set you on a path to live happily, or unhappily, ever after.

Each time you interacted with money, you continued to layer on new lessons, but they all sit on the foundation of your earliest memory. There are three distinct periods in *discovery*—*awareness*, *attention*, and *autonomy*—which occur in succession. The description of these periods will likely cause some memories to come to mind, some of which you have told so many times that the people closest to you could tell them for you! They explain your challenges and triumphs. They are the reasons that you give for not being where you want to be or for an achievement that you want to be modest about. Other stories you may have forgotten will come to mind only because of the new perspective you engage with here. These become part of your story now, with an understanding of your current relationship with money.

*Awareness* begins with your earliest money memory. Your interpretation of this event is the foundation for your relationship with money. Samantha was five when her family moved back to the United States from Spain. She was required to take a test to determine her grade placement in her new elementary school. She was given a picture of coins and asked to identify them. Having no memory of living in the United States, she was not familiar with these coins. As an adult sharing this story with me, she said, "I was a smart kid and could have easily identified currency I was familiar with, but, in this moment, I felt so ashamed because I did not have the answer." She was expected to know these coins.

As we discussed this memory, I asked if the feeling she described from the experience was familiar, and she immediately replied, "Yes!" This showed up in her current relationship with money and was what prompted her to seek my help. Samantha began working with me because she wanted to be independent. She felt that she relied too much on her family but was filled with fear about making mistakes. As an adult, she approached every financial choice with a belief that she was not properly informed and felt shame about her inability to make decisions.

There is a thread that ties your earliest memory to your relationship with money today. Don't be afraid to tug at it! We want this to unravel. Once you find the thread, you will begin to notice how often that young voice of yours runs the conversation.

Brandon remembered being nine when his parents went through a very messy divorce. There was no coordination on his behalf, and unfortunately, he was constantly made aware of the difficulties in his parents' relationship. Brandon's earliest money memory was about a special team jersey that his father bought for him. He treasured it, but when he went to stay at his mother's home on weekends, he was not allowed to bring this jersey with him. His father believed that it would be lost or destroyed at his mother's home. Reflecting on this as an adult, Brandon described valuable items as being easily lost. As he pulled that thread, he shared that all of his thoughts about money were from a position of scarcity. He assumed that he would lose every good career opportunity and that any money he saved would likely disappear if he invested it.

*Awareness* shifts to *attention* with your first financial decision. This is when you possess control over money, and, even though there were adults in your life who guided you, you remember making a choice. Maybe *guided* is a nice way of saying *steered*, *pushed*, or *manipulated*. However, you were given at least the appearance of the opportunity to choose. *Awareness* and *attention* are now in a dance. You gathered information about this thing called money, and it was your turn to do something with it!

Adults often describe their relationship with money to me with broad statements, such as, "I was always a saver. As a kid and teenager, I always held onto money." Or, "Money barely touched my hands. I spent it as soon as I got it." They share these thoughts as if they were genetic facts, coded into their DNA, but the experiences and influencers in their life put them on the path to tend to money in this way.

The experiences that occur in *attention* further develop your relationship with money. Each choice you make has a result. In some cases, it is positive, and others have an undesired outcome. This kind of learning took place throughout your youth and, of course, was not happening only with money. The flow of choice-to-result becomes choice-to-consequence as the decisions become more important. One of the first ways that we understand this relates to behavior within our classrooms. We see how it impacts us socially. In our relationship with money, these lessons don't receive quite the same feedback, and our development continues without adjustment.

*Autonomy* begins when you make *all* of the decisions. The modest control you gained during *attention* was still overseen by adults in your life. The training wheels come off when you begin to earn money. You have responsibilities and obligations. You may seek guidance, but none is actively offered. As you reflect back on this, you may experience a wave of judgment. If you were very young, you may feel like adults let you down by not guiding you. Alternatively, you may burst with pride for taking charge as young as you did. If you are in your twenties, thirties, or forties and feel like you are still beholden to a parent, or now a partner, you may feel resentful. Conversely, you may feel grateful in either of these scenarios. Notice the thoughts that arise and allow them to serve as important information, rather than an emotional block.

Having never been presented with this point of view before, finding this clarity about *autonomy* may be jarring. Notice if you are judging your current relationship with money on a scale of autonomy. Let that go. You are exactly where you belong in this moment. Everything that you learn from *discovery* is truly the best news because it will allow you to understand how you currently operate. To move forward with confidence, you first need to acknowledge where you are. The appropriate action steps to move you forward will be more easily determined once you achieve this clarity.

When the memories are uncovered, and you see the thread to your relationship with money today, you have an opportunity to change the conversation. We can't have five-year-old Samantha making wedding plans and buying a home. She needs to recognize those thoughts and then reposition her thinking to the adult with goals and dreams. When Brandon had a windfall in his business, he came to me to make sure that it wouldn't be lost. Once we uncovered the source of that fear, he was able to move forward with confidence.

I had a conversation with a couple, both in their thirties, who were shopping for a new home. This would be the first time they owned a home, and they struggled to agree on the priorities. Doug grew up in an affluent family and remembered getting to choose anything he wanted for his birthday each year. Yes, you may have guessed it, when he was eight years old, it was a pony!

Maria came from a more modest background. She remembered telling her parents that if they had to choose, it was better to buy a Christmas gift for her younger sister and skip hers. She was seven years old and declared that she understood that money didn't grow on trees! As this couple discussed their home-buying dilemma, Doug talked about a four-bedroom home so they could settle in for the long haul and start their family. Maria thought it would be best to start with a smaller home and continue saving while their family grew. As they talked, it was clear to me I was listening to the debate of an eight- and seven-year-old!

When I shared this with them, they roared with laughter. We were then able to shift the conversation with a new awareness. They listened to each other's concerns with an understanding of the source. They also could consider a variety of other factors in choosing their home. In the end, they chose a home that made it easy for them to commute to work so they could spend more time together as they started a family. That didn't emerge as a priority until they removed those younger voices from the decision process.

Take some time to achieve clarity about your earliest money memory by answering the questions in the *Financial Insight Chapter Guide.* If journaling is your thing, write it out. If you prefer to talk it through, that works too. This exercise is important and will help you shift out of your automated thinking. Don't forget that this memory has been with you for decades. To loosen its grip on your thoughts, you need to shine a bright light on it.

With each choice you make, you are writing the story of your life. Let's make sure that you write with a pen, not a crayon!

CHAPTER 8

# Exploration

Do you remember how great adulthood looked when you were a teenager? Could there be anything more desirable than driving yourself anywhere, staying out as late as you wanted, and calling all the shots? It would be glorious when you finally didn't have to answer to anyone! You would know how to handle everything. You watched your parents and other adults in your life and could see everything they did wrong! You imagined your life and just couldn't wait to get there.

A few short years later, you have brunch with your closest friends and talk about how "adulting sucks" because it's just a lot of responsibilities. You try to hold onto some of your carefree spirit by continuing to party and notice how it interferes with your goals. You've developed a type of self-imposed amnesia that doesn't remember how exciting it all looked now that the experience is not how you imagined it.

Being in your twenties is challenging for many reasons. You reach a level of autonomy, and there is an expectation of *knowing* that begins to grow. You feel as though you should be more savvy. It seems as if others have it all figured out, and you are immersed in a culture of "fake it until you make it." You make decisions about your career and where to live. Your life fills with new people as you meet coworkers, and you may actively date. You form bonds with adult acquaintances and find friends who didn't know you throughout childhood.

In this time period, you are forward-focused, setting goals and trying to find your space in the future. You are finally an adult—this status that you aspired to is happening. Why is it so uncertain and unsatisfying? You think, "I will feel like an adult when..." and you try to fill in the blank with your first "real job" or your first apartment. Those will certainly make you feel like you arrived, right? But they don't. A serious relationship will ground you, right? But it doesn't, and your partner doesn't seem to know what they are doing either!

Your origin story becomes background and shows up in sound bites at parties. But this history is with you all the time. While you emerge into the world as an adult, that past informs every choice you make. Still, you try to find your footing as if that base of knowledge was all behind you. The significant decisions you make in early adulthood set a path. There is a collective misconception that, by virtue of your autonomy, you have everything you need to take these big steps. Your vision of your life from the vantage point of age twenty-five should be clear, right? Anyone in their forties and beyond will read that last sentence and laugh. Those who are younger might feel anxious when they read it. Our collective sense of what happens in early adulthood does not match the reality.

The shift from *discovery* to *growth* doesn't happen on graduation day or with any of your adult firsts. There is a period of transition that we collectively don't acknowledge. *Exploration* begins as you learn about yourself as an adult. In this transition period, you unwittingly write your story with each choice you make. Throughout your twenties and well into your thirties, your decisions come with significant consequences, but the impact may not be in your view at this time. During this period, many opportunities with long-term commitments, like a career, partner, family, and home, become possible. Seeing five or ten years ahead is difficult when you are simply trying to figure out who you are and what you want. And yet the desire to choose and commit to some of the opportunities may be strong. As you think about this period of *exploration*, I need to remind you that the path itself is not problematic. Happiness can be found in life stories of every variety. The problems arise when the path you choose is not based on a deep understanding of yourself.

The decision to start a family is, somewhat surprisingly, one that many folks don't consider to be a financial choice. It is often said, "You can't wait until you can afford children to have them." This is false. Giving it some thought and knowing, in advance, how to fund this twenty-plus-year commitment is very comforting! Similarly, a significant purchase, like buying a home, based solely on the most you can afford is an example of a decision without awareness of what matters most to you. Taking time to learn about yourself should come before these major commitments. Even in routine spending, the paycheck-to-paycheck existence that so many people manage is often caused by a lack of clarity about what is important.

When you reflect back on this period, there will be moments you recognize as good decisions. Those are the ones that moved you forward in a positive way. There will be others that give you pause and make you wonder what you were thinking. If you are in your twenties while reading this, please enjoy this deep-breath moment. You don't need to have it all figured out. You are in *exploration,* and this time doesn't just allow for a slower pace but begs for it. Taking your time to make thoughtful choices is the practice on which you want to focus. When you hurry, you likely make more mistakes. I know that it is difficult to want things and wait. The truth is, however, you are not waiting. You are exploring. Rather than making commitments that you will spend a later decade undoing, use this period of *exploration* to learn about yourself. Let your decisions reside in a deeper understanding. You will set yourself up for success with this way of thinking.

When twenty-six-year-old Sarah looked for an apartment, she had been working with me for a while and knew the amount she felt comfortable spending on rent. She thought that a room in a larger apartment with two or three roommates was the answer. I asked her to tell me more about her ideal home life. She shared that natural light was vital to her wellbeing. She wanted a bedroom that was big enough to accommodate a quiet space to enjoy some solitude. She already lived without much closet space for a few years, so, while improving on that was a "nice to have," it wasn't a deal breaker. With these priorities in mind, the apartment hunt began, and with each space she visited, she struggled to find the most important qualities of light and personal space.

I asked if she looked at any smaller apartments that she could afford on her own. Much to both of our surprise, she hadn't even considered it. Sarah said, "It was like tunnel vision. I thought that I had to have roommates because that's what everyone my age does!" It wasn't long before she came to me with two options. One was an apartment with three roommates, where she would rent the largest bedroom with two closets! The problem was that the window in that room faced another building, and she wouldn't have much light. The other option was a small studio with great windows, a small closet, and slightly lower rent. She needed to make a quick choice because one or both options could be gone within a day. The thoughtful way that she approached this process made it easier to make a decision. Having a space of her own was what she believed she truly wanted, so she opted for the studio. For the next two years, every time we spoke, she said, "If we hadn't talked it through, I would be living with roommates, with no light and spending more just for an unnecessary extra closet!"

During *exploration*, be curious about what brings you happiness. Adjust your thinking away from an arbitrary finish line years ahead and think about the foundation that you can build. The check-the-box life of prior generations does not meet the needs of the twenty-first-century adult. You can create a future that is uniquely yours. *Exploration* is worthy of your time and attention. The fastest way to reach your desired outcome is slowly![6]

If you are beyond your twenties and find yourself wishing for a decade or more back, that isn't necessary. You have the greatest instruction manual for the rest of your life right there in your memory. I promise that the twentysomethings wish they had your point of view, like a crystal ball. Leveraging what you learned begins with a reframing of mistakes to miss-takes. You did exactly what you knew how to do, and you did it with the full consent of a world that expected you to be an instant adult. Your only option was to test your life theories in real time with real choices.

If you are just now becoming aware of the uncomfortable parts of your life, take age out of this conversation completely and embrace that you are in *exploration* now. It is your life and your pace. You don't age out of exploration. You can be there for as long as you want or need.

If you already experienced a jarring moment of realization, in which you felt enough adulting pain to seek help, or if there are clear miss-takes, it is likely that *exploration* is complete, and you are ready to move forward. Perhaps you sought help for a while, but each book you read and podcast you listened to was more of the same. No one ever told you that you were *exploring* in search of *freedom* on your way to *growth.*

---

6 André De Shields, June 9, 2019, Tony Awards Acceptance Speech, The 73rd Annual Tony Awards, New York City.

CHAPTER 9

# Freedom

Financial freedom is a phrase in need of a reboot. It is typically used in marketing or the media to describe a sort of endgame in which money no longer matters. The absurdity of that messaging prevents you from accessing freedom in the proper place in your story. The notion that money ceases to matter if you have an endless supply doesn't make sense. You still have to make daily choices about how to use the money. As a matter of fact, the challenges you face now become even more intense if you continue with the same behaviors using more money. The quantity of money available does not determine your level of freedom. You access freedom in your decision process.

The definition of freedom is:

> free·dom /ˈfrēdəm/ (*noun*) – the power or right to act, speak, or think as one wants without hindrance or restraint.[7]

Now, let's infuse that definition with your money and take a deeper dive into the meaning:

> (financial) freedom – your power and right to earn, spend, and/or save as you want without hindrance or restraint.

---

7 "freedom, n," Oxford Languages and Google, Oxford University Press, March 2023, web, accessed February 5, 2023.

As an adult with autonomy over money:

1. You possess **the power and right to earn, spend, and/or save**.

This is a fact of life. Whether or not you exercise the power or right to achieve your dreams is your choice. With each decision you make and each action you take, you assert your power and right. There are no exceptions, so let's address the ones you might want to claim.

- Earning – If you choose to rely on a spouse/partner or anyone else to support you financially, you use your power to make that choice.
- Spending – In whatever way you spend money, you assert your right to use the funds available to you.
- Saving – If you are not saving for the future, this happens within your power.

2. You determine the use of money **as you want** it to be.

If you have not been effective in directing money toward what is most important to you, there may be *shoulds* that cloud your thoughts and get in the way. The perceived obstacles do not negate your authority to make choices that fulfill your wants and needs, even if you struggle to do so.

3. You act **without hindrance or restraint**.

Any circumstances that appear to prevent you from taking action are in your way because you have not removed them. If you believe that you cannot alter your circumstances, it is because you are, in some way, unwilling to make the needed changes.

*Freedom* exists the moment you assert your power and right to move money in the direction of your best life. Resetting freedom from a future event to the present moment is the most powerful step on your journey. You will need to repeat this step many times before it becomes natural. Because the idea of *financial freedom* has been used to diminish our current circumstances for so long, this reset requires your attention and an intention to make the shift. Each time you recognize that your current choices determine the future, you access the state of *freedom*.

Imagine a doorway under a sign that reads, "Enter Here for Freedom." What is on the other side of that doorway for you? Now, before you respond, I want an honest answer. Don't say piles of money and no responsibility. This isn't a bank heist! I want you to think about your best life. Where would you live? What kind of work would you do? Who would be in your life? Would you travel or have certain leisure activities in your regular routine? Once you define your best life, I have a more difficult question for you. What are you willing to do to achieve that vision? It is your willingness that enables you to begin moving in that direction and allows you to cross the threshold of *freedom*. You have the power and right to make that dream a reality. It may require time and changes, but it is yours to pursue. Any hindrance or restraint that you perceive is yours to change.

When I created FIT, I already had a thriving business. Carter CPA LLC (CCPA) was a successful tax and accounting firm. Some of my clients had been with me for over thirty years, while new clients showed up in my inbox daily. I could easily grow CCPA and, by many measures, achieve greater levels of success. Unfortunately, the idea of growing this business did not appeal to me. I was often stressed and overwhelmed. The deadlines and volume of work were too much. Continuing this path meant that I would need to hire more staff to ease the burden. This sounds like a really good problem for a business owner, doesn't it? I could make a lot more money and ultimately oversee a large firm if

I wanted. I grappled with this for quite a while. The part of the work I enjoyed the most, talking with people about their lives and helping them make the best choices, would not be feasible if the quantity of tax preparation continued to increase.

For me, *freedom* would not be found in higher revenue from a larger accounting firm. I wanted to find a way to make coaching, not tax preparation, my primary source of revenue. I wanted to spend my days doing the work of FIT. If I could replace CCPA with FIT, I would live my best life. The question I had to answer was, "Am I willing to take the steps to change my business?" I already had the experience of paying down debt and adjusting my spending to fulfill my dream of living in New York City. Was I ready to step through another doorway to *freedom*? The answer was, "Yes, no matter how long it takes, I will work day by day, decision by decision, to achieve this dream."

*Freedom* occurs the moment you make the choice to pursue your best life. It influences the decisions and action steps that will occur in the following phase of *growth*. There are two ways that the opportunity for *freedom* presents itself: *freedom by consequences* or *freedom by design*.

When *exploration* concludes, an awareness of self that did not exist before arises. This awareness is the first sign that you are ready for *freedom*. You no longer question what you want but instead wonder how to achieve it. The way that you perceive your current circumstances impacts your belief about the possibility of achieving your dreams. If you believe you are in a difficult position, feelings of fear, shame, or regret impact your thoughts about money. If you believe you are doing okay but don't know your next steps, feelings of uncertainty take over your thoughts about money. You describe your circumstances through the lens of a question that you don't know how to answer or a perceived problem. The challenge may be negative or positive. Some of the most common ones include the following:

- Struggles with debt,
- Fear about investing,

- A breakup or divorce,
- An upcoming engagement or cohabitation,
- Loss of a job,
- A career opportunity,
- Health issues, and
- An inheritance.

All of these circumstances require you to make a decision. The circumstances call you to action. You are aware that the decision will have consequences. A miss-take at this stage of your life seems far more precious than in your earlier years. There is a sense that you could do some irreversible damage now. You seek help but aren't sure who to trust.

This moment is pivotal. Life flings open the door, showing you an opportunity for *freedom,* and you can either make a choice that asserts your power or delays it. The choice you make will determine outcomes that surpass this one decision. If you don't adopt a thoughtful approach, considering lessons from the past and being honest about what you truly want, you will likely experience more and more challenging circumstances. While you try to find the best path, it may seem like you don't have access to *freedom* because you lack the preparation and skills needed to make a decision with confidence.

When you are unprepared and forced into decision-making, you experience the opportunity of *freedom by consequences.* This is both the most common way and the least desirable way to access *freedom.* It is more difficult to find the answers that move you forward toward a desired outcome, but it is the open door. If you choose to step through that doorway, you will have to do the work of being honest with yourself, having difficult conversations with loved ones, and changing behaviors that impede your happiness. *Freedom* is available in the assertion of your power to make a choice that is best for you. Making that choice in this type of circumstance is daunting.

Carol and Tyler were recently married, and each had credit card debt. They reached out to me after friends told them about FIT. They wanted to buy a home and start a family, but they couldn't see how that would be possible. In our first conversation, I learned about their aspirations, but they didn't have any financial information to share with me. We planned next steps for another conversation to review the details of the debt and other financial facts. I didn't hear from them again for two years.

The second time that they reached out, they seemed more determined and asked if I would help them create a plan. I asked what prompted them to circle back after so much time passed. They shared that they had tried on their own and made no progress. Now that Tyler received a raise in his salary, they really wanted to focus and move in the right direction. I explained that there was work to do in reviewing their financial data as well as at the behaviors that kept them from making progress. We planned next steps, but, again, they disappeared for two more years.

When they reached out for the third time, their situation had worsened significantly. Their debt was more than double what it had been when we first spoke. They declared they were finally ready to take this on. I asked them what was different this time. Carol shared that they were expecting their first child. They were terrified because they couldn't afford childcare, and their apartment was too small for their growing family. They wanted to move but couldn't qualify to buy a home because of their debt. Even moving to a larger apartment was overwhelming due to the cost of a move. They now faced tremendous pressure and had no idea how to solve any of the various issues.

They said they would gather all of the information and do anything I recommended if I could help them figure this out. I told them that there was only one question they had to answer. "Are you willing to do the work?" For four years, they said they wanted to make changes but were unwilling to take the steps needed. Even with the increase in income, the lack of attention to their behaviors made their circumstances worse. The consequences of delaying put them in a more difficult position. If we had started the work years before, this would have been a happy time for them. Instead, they were starting a family while feeling fear, shame, and regret. The opportunity for *freedom* was always available, but they waited until the possible consequences became dire.

Waiting for the opportunity of *freedom by consequences* is like walking through a long corridor filled with doors. At any moment, a door can fling open, and you will be pulled through to circumstances you need to manage. How well you deal with these circumstances is a function of your willingness to assert your power. This determines if you move closer to your best life or if you return to the corridor to wait, unprepared, for the next challenge. Carol and Tyler saw the first door when they learned about FIT. They saw the second door when Tyler got a raise. It wasn't until their first child was on the way that they found the consequences compelling enough to choose a new path.

The more desirable path is *freedom by design*. Instead of a corridor with doors, imagine an open space with archways. You can see the possibilities and are prepared to make choices when opportunities present themselves. Even unforeseen circumstances, like an illness, don't shake the stability you set in place. Shifting from being reactive to being proactive is the difference between *freedom by consequences* and *freedom by design.*

When you align your present actions with your past lessons and future dreams, you use *financial insight* to unlock *freedom. Financial insight* is a deep, intuitive understanding of your values and an accurate knowledge of your data. It is this heightened awareness that allows you to clearly see where you are today, understand the lessons of the past, and define the desired path forward. It is a skill to look back at the choices that worked well and know how to access that kind of thinking again, as well as look at the decisions that didn't work out and see them as a source for deeper personal understanding. *Freedom by design* is a path you can choose right now.

When Justin and Lynn decided to end their marriage, they agreed to focus on the easiest possible transition for their son. They wanted to complete the divorce process quickly, without letting the emotional aspects cloud their better judgment. Soon after they began the divorce process, Lynn told Justin that she was uncomfortable with her attorney and wanted to make a change. Justin shared that he wasn't feeling great about his choice either. They each had received advice about how to "win the most money." When they met with me for the first time, together, they asked if I could guide them to a fair and objective financial division. I told them I didn't know any other way! The plan we established allowed Justin and Lynn to thoughtfully prepare for the next chapter. We discussed what they each envisioned for their post-marriage life. Rather than spend a significant amount on legal fees, we used the money they had to make their desired outcomes a reality. Lynn went back to school and started a new career. Justin bought a new home and remarried.

Whenever I work with couples in this situation, I remind them that the objective is to leverage the lessons learned, define a vision of the future, and use all of that information to create the best outcome in the present. This sets them up for the *freedom* they seek by getting divorced. In fact, I have the very same conversation with newly engaged couples too.

To access *freedom by design*, shift your mindset to see this next chapter as resetting your life based on all you know about yourself today. The timeline is not a concern in *freedom* because this is about making the choice in the present moment. There is no finish line to race toward, and the more time you spend in this inquiry, the happier you will be throughout your life. Instead of enduring pressure to launch a career, find a partner, or start a family, shift your focus to *exploration* and truly knowing yourself. With that knowledge, you can prepare to choose a desired path forward without hindrance or restraint.

If you are already years into a career, relationship, or home, this is a time for reflection. Do some honest pondering about what makes you happy and what keeps you from happiness. The focus on *freedom* allows you to lead with your values so that each time you make a choice, you consider what matters most to you. It illuminates the *shoulds* as soon as they creep into your thoughts. These skills require practice.

The principal difference between *freedom by consequences* and *freedom by design* is whether you are forced through this doorway of opportunity or seek it. Either way, you can be successful. By starting today, you can accomplish this in the least disruptive and most productive way. By delaying or avoiding your finances until life hands you a circumstance, you risk the perpetuation of stress and struggle. It could lead to more miss-takes and a longer period of recovery before you can pursue what you truly want.

I first observed this quality of preparedness in clients who consistently made great choices, routinely moving their lives forward in the best ways. They were both pleased with the present circumstances and were on track to achieve the outcomes they desired for the future. This reset of your understanding of *freedom*, the power and right to act as you want without hindrance or restraint, makes the action steps that follow in *growth* possible.

CHAPTER 10

# Growth

*Growth* is a chapter in which you establish the best path forward by taking thoughtful action steps. Whether you walk through the doorway of *freedom by design* or are flung headfirst by consequences, crossing that threshold brings you to the opportunity for *growth*. In my experience, I observed too many people who didn't make it to this phase. They got stuck in an earlier chapter. Some made one or more choices during *exploration* that caused them to believe their circumstances couldn't be altered. For others, there was a lack of willingness to assert *freedom*. Our collective approach of racing to retirement caused a blur through the opportunity for a brilliant reset for many people. Being the author of your story, day by day, choice by choice, is the reality, whether you are mindful of it or not. You write your life story. When you seize the opportunity of *growth*, you strive to achieve a level of mastery in the work of *financial insight*.

*Growth* takes the inquiry of *freedom* to the next level. It transforms your definition of success into action steps to achieve your vision. Remember, no two people with the same amount of money live the exact same life. Success is deeply personal. Only you can determine what your best life looks like. You may have some elements of it now, and others may seem impossible. You may hesitate to articulate this out of fear that it is not attainable. Keep in mind that having it all is not the same as having all of it! When you define what you truly want in your life, you also let go of pressures to have things that are not important to you.

When I was in my twenties, I believed that I wanted a big, beautiful home. People around me seemed to value this, and I took that cue. When I needed some inspiration, I drove around neighborhoods that looked like this dream. At the time, this inspired me, and I remember thinking, "That is what success looks like." It wasn't until my friend pointed out how happy I was when I spent time in New York City that I realized my long-time definition of success didn't belong to me. When I moved from my townhouse in New Jersey to my apartment in Manhattan, I cut the size of my living space in half. Another friend of mine, who lives in a large home, once referred to my move as downsizing. I shared with her that, for me, this was an enormous upsizing because I had the whole city on my doorstep!

Success, defined by you, rather than the media, marketing, or even your inner circle, is where you want to focus. If your home brings you the comfort you desire, there is no upgrade needed. If your work is fulfilling without pressure, you don't need a promotion. If you aspire to be CEO of a Fortune 500 company, go for it. If you desire more time with your family and that means less income, there is nothing wrong with that choice. If being debt-free and traveling is your best life, declare that dream, and it will be your guide. While you dream, avoid being too precious about getting it right. What you envision for your future will likely change over time, but the vision is needed to pull you forward. Your dreams will evolve. Plan to keep dreaming as you take action steps.

As you might expect, *growth* may include some growing pains. As your definition of success becomes clearer, you may find that you are not heading in the direction of what you truly want. The changes that you need to make may feel inspiring, but it is possible that they may also be daunting. Many people stop here, never taking the action steps that move them closer to their dream. They believe they stay safely in their "comfort zone," but there is a tricky nuance here that we need to address. You may be confusing your comfort zone and your discomfort zone. In your discomfort zone, you wish for things to be different but hold onto the status quo because making the change feels difficult. By doing this, you actively avoid what you want. With an awareness of your discomfort zone, you can shift your attention to the desired outcome and take action steps with more ease. Remember how James initially experienced his spending as comfort? The alternative was to work on the habits and implement a plan to pay off debt and save. He struggled for a bit and then later recognized his spending and increasing debt was the source of his stress and struggle.

The comfort zone and discomfort zone confusion isn't always as extreme as it was for James. Many of us can identify with the self-medicating of shopping or other vices. A favorite example of this is what I call "tired takeout." You have a refrigerator filled with food, but you are tired and don't feel like preparing any of it. You order takeout, and while you wait for it to arrive, a little guilt creeps in. You justify your decision as a reward for all you do and let the guilt go. After eating, you still think about what you spent and the groceries that may spoil. It is as if your last bite was the unwanted dessert of regret! Distinguishing between the comfort zone and discomfort zone takes practice. You can check in with yourself by asking, "Is my current action in service of my comfort in this moment or of the dream that I am working toward?" The more action steps you take toward your definition of success, the more likely you can answer that question by saying, "Both!"

Determining if you are on a path that is taking you where you want to be or keeping you from it is the next step. By this point in life, you have responsibilities and obligations to yourself and others, so a thoughtful process is needed. For some, this will mean ending a relationship or finding one. A career change might be needed, and the pivot might require time. A different home or a new location might be important to move you forward literally and figuratively. Taking action steps to be on the path toward your definition of success is not about abrupt change. When you step out of your discomfort zone to change your path, this is the process of *course correction.*

Tom and Alex were saving for a down payment on a second home. They owned their apartment in an outer borough of New York City and wanted a getaway upstate. They believed a nearby escape from city life would be great because their jobs kept them from traveling as much as they wanted. They also hoped to have a space that allowed them to entertain friends and family. They put a lot of pressure on themselves to save enough to buy this second home within two years. When they shared the stress they experienced to reach this goal, I found it troubling. They immediately protested when I suggested that they expand the timeline because they didn't want to wait more than a few years to achieve this dream.

We worked through the decision process to make sure they planned for all of the related costs. They considered furnishing the new home but hadn't given much thought to needing a car. They were unsure which town they were most interested in and were planning to choose a location based on what they could afford in the shortest period of time. Whenever there is urgency around a goal, I see red flags. This is typically a sign that you are not on the right track, and slowing down to be more thoughtful will be beneficial.

After asking a series of questions, I pointed out that they had not mentioned anything about wanting to own another home. They were puzzled and asked how else they could make this work. Knowing how demanding their jobs were, I asked how often they thought they would use the property. Again, they hadn't fully considered this. I asked if they ever thought about renting just during the weekends or weeks that they could get away. They had not considered this option at all.

Based on the amount they already saved for a down payment and furniture, they would be able to rent far more beautiful homes than they planned to buy. I suggested that they try this out for the upcoming summer and fall. This was an opportunity to experience different towns and determine how often they could spend time away from the city. They also could get a feel for the transportation without a car and sometimes rent a car. They could entertain and see how their friends and family responded to invitations. Best of all, the timeline shortened because they could start this immediately. Tom and Alex often talk about this life-changing clarification of their goal. By year three, they realized that being near their friends was the true priority that they didn't previously understand. They sold their apartment and moved to a neighborhood in Manhattan where most of their friends lived. Had they spent all of the money they saved for a new home, this move wouldn't have been possible.

In *growth,* you choose actions that lead you to desired outcomes. You do this with a deeper understanding of who you are and what matters most to you, but stay curious. Tom and Alex knew that they wanted something, but it wasn't until they actively worked on the goal that they gained full clarity. To ensure that the path you are on leads you to your definition of success, state your dreams with specific dates. When you choose a date, it is not to create a deadline but instead to help you determine if your plan is realistic. The date that Tom and Alex initially chose created pressure, which helped us reveal that the plan might not be quite right. It was the choosing of the date that generated more questions. "Someday" dreams rarely happen. When you choose a real date, month/day/year, you can work backwards to see if your plan works. You can design action steps and benchmarks along the way that allow you to track your progress.

*Growth* occurs when you establish your personal definition of success and take action to reach that vision. Keep in mind that you have decades of thoughts, habits, and behaviors that are almost automatic. What you are doing now is practicing. That is why *course correction* is a process. Take your time to reflect on all of the lessons from the past.

The miss-takes provide you with a wealth of information for future choices. As you practice using this deeper understanding of yourself in your decision-making process, you will reach a level of intuition that feels more and more natural. Your financial facts, the data, are the final pieces of this puzzle. An accurate knowledge of your income and spending, along with management of debt and a plan for accumulation, all come together to give you the confidence of *financial insight*. In *growth*, you will recover from the challenges created by earlier decisions. Each decision you make now will create a new set of circumstances. Now, you are writing the life story that you want to tell.

CHAPTER 11

# Harmony and Independence

After you clarify your vision, make the needed course corrections, and choose a path forward, you are done, right? Nope! You are just getting to the best part. You are making decisions with confidence. Your values, what matters most to you, are considered without the noise of *shoulds* distracting you. Together with your knowledge of your financial facts, you are empowered with this new skill to align these two key factors. The course corrections of *growth* may still be a work in progress, but you can see your dreams becoming reality on a well-planned timeline. Before you buy a new home, complete the career shift, or pay off the debt, you experience a new way to measure success. Your level of ease, stability, confidence, and freedom become your focus.

At this stage of your *financial insight* journey, you notice misalignments much quicker than in the past. You are a multifaceted person, and you crave solutions when things feel like they are not working in the best possible way. Before seeking a solution, it is important to be sure that you aim to solve the right problem! A bidirectional approach to this type of inquiry allows you to see more varied options. Let's look at some examples.

If you struggle to pay your rent or mortgage, ask both if your career supports the home you have *and* if the home you have is appropriate for the career path that you chose. If you only ask the first question, you may conclude that you are not making enough money. The solution could be the pursuit of a second job or working toward a promotion. The second question causes you to consider an alternate view. If your home creates financial pressure and you are happy in your work, determining the action steps needed to reduce your home costs is the issue that needs your attention.

If you have stressful conversations about spending with your partner/family, you can ask if your income supports the choices you made about your partner and family *and* how you influence the way your partner or family use your income. You may be avoiding some uncomfortable conversations with your partner/family. These answers may reveal the need for more course correction. Too often, families think that more income will reduce stress, but it is even more likely that thoughtful conversations and small adjustments based on values will achieve the impact you seek.

If you aren't participating in leisure activities or find vacations stressful, ask if you spend time enjoying hobbies, leisure, adventure, and vacation *and* if you find enjoyment in the activities you choose. Recognizing an unfulfilled desire will open up new opportunities. If you skip activities that matter to you because they leave you feeling guilty or regretful, adjustments may be needed to make those activities enjoyable.

*Harmony* is defined as "a consistent, orderly, or pleasing arrangement of parts."[8] Imagine your life as a pleasing arrangement of parts! Why isn't this the title of every commencement speech?! It's a much more helpful direction than "be successful." Achieving *harmony* becomes a natural desire when you truly understand what matters most to you. It might be a short path to *harmony* if your work in *growth* answered many of the questions. Checking in on each of your values with a bidirectional view will confirm that you move along the best path forward or will reveal more work to be done.

---

8 Dictionary.com, January 30, 2023, https://www.dictionary.com/browse/harmony.

*Harmony* brings about a level of comfort that was not available in the earlier phases. Your awareness about any undesirable obligations is handled with far greater ease. Achieving *independence* means that you can make any choice without causing a major disturbance in *harmony*. You have put yourself in a position where you can change your job or end a relationship and still take care of yourself. Your choices are fully your own. Now, before you think that I'm suggesting a moment where you dismantle your life and move on, note that you *can* make any choice. The achievement of *independence* is the *ability* to choose.

Choose the partner you are with because you want to be with them. Choose the job you are in because it is the work you want to do. Provide for your children based on what you want to give them. By this point, you've defined success, you learned the skills of *financial insight*, and you took the steps of course correction. If you have done all of this with honesty, true *independence* will be choosing exactly where you are. However, it is the ability to make the choice that is the focus.

Jill has been unhappily married for twenty years and considered divorce at least a dozen times. In the early years of her marriage, her spouse supported the family with his job alone, and she was able to be the mom she wanted to be to their children. She loved to travel and was able to do so as much as she wanted. She considered that to be her way of finding balance with the challenges of her relationship. As the kids became teenagers, her spouse lost his well-paying job, and they began to struggle financially. Her unhappiness in the relationship was now compounded by limitations on travel and the growing debt to keep the kids in their activities.

She returned to work, but after so many years out of the workforce, her job, along with her spouse's new job, was not fully supplementing the loss of income. The spending that took place over these two decades was done with the assumption that the income would continue to grow, not shrink. There was never a focus on savings because so much was spent to soothe the unhappiness. Jill sought my help because, now, in her fifties with two kids heading into college, the financial pressure consumed her. She believed that there was no way out and that any course correction would upend all of their lives. The possibility of *independence* is out of reach for Jill at this time. She is learning lessons from the past as she defines what success will look like when she emerges from the current circumstances. She understands that this is the story she has been writing and is taking action to change the path. While this may seem like an extreme example, many people find themselves with no access to *independence.* Spending to soothe unhappiness, leading to debt and limited savings, is epidemic. Your ability to achieve *independence* begins with the choices you make today.

Each of the prior chapters in your story are necessary to achieve the self-awareness and attain the skills needed to reach the level of confidence that exists for *independence.* Based on this understanding of the steps needed to reach *independence,* it becomes clear that the pressure placed on emerging adults is an unfair burden.

This is the challenge that my twenty-five-year-old nephew, Scott, expressed when he compared his life to mine. In sharing with him where I was at twenty-five, he began to see that he is on a good path. However, it wasn't enough to demonstrate that he will achieve *independence*, probably much sooner than I did.

We took our conversation a step further in talking about one of his goals. He is an artist and dreams of having a studio space so that he doesn't have to paint in his apartment. Based on his financial data, he could fulfill this dream today, but he decided to wait so he could accomplish some other milestones first. He set a goal for growth in his job and his income. He is also thinking about the steps that he and his partner will take in their relationship in the coming years. Before he adds the expense of an art studio, he wants to make sure that his desire for stability, one of his core values, is fulfilled in every area of his life. His thoughtful approach in *exploration* will likely mean less course correcting later and will lead him to *independence* on the fast track.

Both Jill and Scott can make their way to *independence*. Their paths are very different. The ability to move through each chapter is only possible when you begin where you are, today. Your age is not relevant, and your current circumstances are the only possible starting point. Accept the story you have written thus far, envision where you want to go, and then, choice by choice, write with intention.

CHAPTER 12

# Joy

*Joy* is defined as the emotion evoked by well-being, success, or the prospect of possessing what one desires.[9] This is not a one-size-fits-all accomplishment. Also, it is not a distant point in the future.

To help you understand *joy*, let's first talk about its opposite. In the early 1990s, the FIRE movement was introduced. FIRE stands for "Financial Independence, Retire Early." This plan has you save 50 to 75 percent of your income with the aim of retiring in your thirties or forties.[10] Mitch was the first person to share this plan with me, and I thought he was kidding. He already spent a few years in a high-pressure job and had given up everything he loved to do. He boasted about the savings he accumulated by the age of thirty while he described himself as exhausted and miserable. He came to me because he wanted to confirm that he was on track to retire by his goal of forty. I wasn't convinced that he showed up to ask me to do the math. It seemed unlikely because he could do that himself.

I sensed that he wanted approval, or maybe disapproval. I was baffled by his enthusiasm for the plan while he described his unhappy existence. I asked, "What is the dream? If you retire at forty, what do you want to do with the rest of your life?"

---

9 Merriam-Webster, January 17, 2023, https://www.merriam-webster.com/dictionary/joy.

10 Playing with Fire, "FIRE Explained," January 20, 2023, https://www.playingwithfire.co/whatisfire.

He stared at me blankly. "I won't have to work. I can do anything."

"You've spent years working, with minimal time for relationships, family, and friends. No vacations or hobbies. You are hyper-focused on a future that you can't describe. If you spend the next decade in this bubble, what will you have learned about yourself? How will you know what to do next?" I paused. "Do you want to further delay figuring out who you are? Do you want to spend another decade focused only on producing income?"

The race to an arbitrary finish line is in direct conflict with the natural process of life. No matter your age today, imagine yourself at ninety, reflecting back on your life. Assume you are in reasonably good health, your mind is sharp, you still have your sense of humor, and you know how your whole story unfolded. From this perspective, you see the chapters of *discovery, growth,* and *joy*. You tell the stories of transition that reveal how you *explored* and found *freedom*. You remember when you achieved *harmony* and true *independence*. The mistakes you made and the challenges of course correction tie all of the chapters together. You describe how your choices were the catalyst for every consequence. Whether you achieved the dreams of your younger days or are in a position that you did not anticipate, it is clear that you were the author of the story. While it happened, it seemed like the circumstances pushed and pulled you, but in the end, you know it was always by your decisions that the story was written.

My grandfather, Arnie, passed just a month before his ninetieth birthday. He was the same sharp and funny guy right up until the end. He lived a beautiful life, filled with happiness and, sometimes, struggles. He never had wealth, but he never strived for that either. Being able to support his family and watch television was pretty much all he needed. I don't know what he dreamed of as a young man because he never shared that. I was twenty-seven years old when he passed, and while I asked a lot of questions, I regret that I never inquired about his dreams. I do have some hints that help me know he was satisfied with how his life turned out, though.

He found my drive for my career amusing and often compared me to his father. Great-Grandpa Joe was a tailor who worked well into his nineties. He would come home late and apologize to his family, "I'm sorry. I had another pair of pants to finish."

During Grandpa Arnie's final years, he lived with my parents, and I still lived at home too. There were many days during tax season when I came home late. "What happened? You had another pair of pants?!" Grandpa teased. He didn't like that I worked so much. "It's not your company. Why do you work so hard?"

"It will be mine someday. I want to take care of people in my own way. I want to really help and not have a boss to answer to," I replied.

He shrugged and said, "I never cared that much." We laughed together and understood that each of us must find our own way. "Good for you. I'm glad you know what you want," he concluded.

Grandpa Arnie worked for the Elias Sports Bureau and for the US Postal Service. I remember visiting him in his last job as a mailroom clerk in an office building when I was about ten years old. What struck me the most was how happy people were to see him as he moved from office to office. They all knew my name as I walked with him. He had gotten to know everyone, asked about their families, and shared about his own. He found joy in his work, joy in his family, and joy in his hobbies, and all without a frantic pursuit of money.

Old age and retirement are not prerequisites for *joy*. This phase can be attained long before old age and without pressure and chaos as the path. If you choose to work for the love of the work itself, or because the income provides you with what you want and need in other areas of your life, that will be part of *joy* for you. I describe the FIRE movement as the opposite of *joy* because that kind of plan robs you of the years that are most important for building a foundation for happiness. Learning about yourself during *discovery* and *exploration* and seizing the opportunities of *freedom* and *growth* are far too important to skip. By using all of that information to define what success means to you, a true personal definition, you will achieve *joy.*

Once Mitch began to understand that his priorities were scalded by FIRE, he sought real guidance from me. He recognized that he tried to jump from *discovery* to *joy.* Because of his savings, he was able to make a change, but I encouraged him to do it slowly and thoughtfully. Just changing jobs and spending haphazardly was not an appropriate course correction. It would be worth it to spend time being curious about what was most important to him. Over the next decade, he worked in five different companies, looking for work that he really liked.

Along the way, he met a partner and bought a home. By the time he was forty-five, he found work that inspired him in a field that required him to obtain another degree. At fifty-five, he thrived in his career and never talked of retirement. "I think I would have been bored and burned through the money quickly if I had stayed on that path," he said, reflecting on the twenty-five years we worked together. That was not the intention of FIRE, but it would have been ironic! In each phase of a pressure-filled plan like FIRE, you burn something down.

My biggest inspiration for *financial insight* came from Simone and Nick. They had already achieved *joy* when I met them over thirty years ago. They were clients when I began working with Robert and were quick to embrace me. Simone especially took on the role of a mentor to me. They both had thriving careers, and, being in their forties, there was no limit to what they could each achieve. They knew everything about their finances, and working with them was so easy. They focused on what brought them happiness, like travel and skiing. They skillfully saved for the future while enjoying the present. In addition to their home in New York City, they bought another home at the beach and a third in an up-and-coming ski resort town. When those areas became more popular, they sold those homes and moved on to the next venture. It seemed like everything they touched turned to gold. They were offered many opportunities for investments that didn't interest them, so they passed with no fear of missing out. All the while, they were happy and at ease with every choice they made.

"Simone, how do you make so many great decisions?" I once asked.

"Thoughtfully, without any *shoulds*," she replied. I studied every move this couple made. They were in their early fifties when Simone called to say, "Nick decided to stop working, and I'm thinking about selling my business."

"Why?" I asked.

"We believe that we have enough money to be happy. If it doesn't work out, we can work again, but we know we can never get this time back." She sold her business, and they began a new life. They stayed in New York City part of the time and spent the rest of the year traveling. They found another home that they loved, again in ski country. A number of years later, they sold both of their homes to live on the west coast in a smaller city because they liked the arts community there. With every adventure, I could see how they took thoughtful steps. If a project interested them, they didn't mind consulting work but never again worked just for the sake of earning money. Over the years I observed Simone and Nick, I compared them to other clients who were the same age and had much more money than they did, but struggled. The difference that I found was that those who struggled consistently made decisions that caused them to stay stuck without ever reaching *growth*.

Just a few years ago, twenty years after they stopped working, Simone and Nick decided they wanted to sell their home and move somewhere they had never lived before. Having traveled to many places in Europe over the years, they chose an area in Spain that felt like a great fit for who they were now, in their seventies. After decades of living well and making great choices throughout their lives, *joy* gave Simone and Nick access to a new cycle beginning with *discovery* once again. Looking back over all of their choices, I realized that they had done this when they stopped working and with each following move they made. The cyclic nature of life, like the changing of seasons, is true of our relationship with money too. If Simone and Nick subscribed to the view of beginning, middle, and end, they would have never lived this extraordinary life. It was their innate understanding of *financial insight* that allowed them to consistently achieve the most desirable outcomes again and again.

In *joy*, you have the most empowered relationship with money. Some dreams come true faster than others. Some dreams are only established after you reach others. I have lived in my dream location for eight years now. When I moved here, I thought this was all I could ever want. As I find myself dreaming about what is next, I can share from my personal experience that *joy* exists in the ability to be curious and intentionally move to another chapter of *discovery*. Learning more about myself allowed me to see that coaching, writing, and speaking about *financial insight* was what I wanted next for my career. That *discovery* led me back through the cycle.

It was a difficult course correction, to let go of some of my accounting business and the success that Grandpa Arnie watched me work so hard to accomplish. Recognizing that it was no longer the best path for me, I let go of nice clients, ones I loved and had worked with for decades. I assured them that I would be here for them if they needed coaching, the work that inspires me, but for the tax and accounting services, I found them a new firm. In the pursuit of my best life, I was able to find a way forward that took care of me and those that I cared about most.

With each choice you make, you bring yourself closer to or farther away from your dreams. Your story is written, not to accomplish a singular happily ever after but instead to build the foundation for another chapter, another cycle.

# Part III

# Writing Your Next Chapter

CHAPTER 13

# Preparing for Success

Are you ready to get to work? With your new awareness, I invite you to be gentle with yourself as you take your next steps. Consider first that you don't need to change anything, and you certainly don't need to change everything. There might be some changes that you desire. Work on just one at a time. Remember that in your relationship with money, you have years, or decades, of practice thinking and acting a particular way. You and money may need a little couples counselling to work out your issues! Trying to move too fast or doing too much will not create an environment for success. To help you begin the mindset shift, I want to highlight some common pitfalls.

In the past, you may have been intrigued by anything that promised a quick fix or seemed like a get-rich-quick scheme. This is the *shortcut pitfall*. Even in a circumstance where a sudden increase in money is available, like an inheritance or winning the lottery (yes, I worked with two lottery winners), the process does not change. There is no shortcut. In those extreme circumstances, the recipient has two options. They can pause, reflect, and make sure they make the best decisions, including habit change and course correction, or they can continue as they were and likely make similar miss-takes on a larger scale.

Adam came to work with me when he landed his second role on Broadway. I thought he would be excited at our first meeting, but instead, he was terrified. "I spent everything I earned when I landed that first gig. I have nothing left from the highest-earning period of my life." At that time, he assumed he would more easily land a role in another show, and would continue to work consistently, at this new level of income. When the first show closed, he had no work for over three years. He struggled and was embarrassed as he took any catering job he could find just to pay rent. He wanted to make sure he didn't repeat his past mistake. He had been in this new role for a few weeks and set aside part of his earnings, but he wasn't sure if it was enough or what to do with it. He had incurred debt over the past few years. He thought he should pay that off first and then start saving.

Adam was twenty-eight at the time and still learning about himself and what he wanted in his life. This was a period of *exploration. Freedom by consequences* was beckoning. He began to relax when I shared that the lessons from the past were already helping him to determine the next steps. We talked about his goals for his career and his plans to get engaged to his partner soon. We looked at his data, including the amount he earned, his current expenses, and the debt that needed to be managed. In our first meeting, the only outcome necessary was a mindset shift. He needed to slow down and allow us to create a thoughtful plan. Paying off the debt without saving would put him in the same position as before.

Adam needed to look at the way he was spending, consider adjustments, and then course correct. One step at a time, one decision at a time. We worked on his relationship with money and habit changes over the following months. When his contract was coming to an end, Adam was clear about his plan. He not only sought a renewal of the contract but asked to be considered for a bigger part in the show that paid more. With another year in the same role, his debt would be paid off, and he would have savings that made him feel stable. If he was able to get the promotion, he would also be ready to get engaged and plan a wedding in one year. The confidence that he gained in his finances spilled right into his career. The promotion came a few months later, and his plan was in motion.

The *postpone pitfall* occurs when you believe that you don't have time to focus on your finances. Having read this book, you are now aware this is just a little lie that you tell yourself. Before you knew the truth—your story is written with every choice you make—you could plan to work on this someday. That is no longer possible. You may want to spend time judging the past or wishing you started sooner. That wallowing does not move you forward! The past lessons serve you well when you learn from them. The only time that you are starting too late is tomorrow! All there is to do is to start now. If you don't begin the work, you choose to write a story of struggle, stress, and uncertainty.

Paul and Sharon are in their eighties now. They were clients of my accounting firm for over thirty years. They belonged to fancy social clubs, dined in the best restaurants, and always dressed beautifully. They entertained friends in their apartment and traveled frequently. From the outside, they appeared to live a good life, but from my vantage point, I knew that they were always in trouble. They consistently spent more money than they earned, and their debt was always increasing. The moment they received any extra income, they paid off the debt and called it a fresh start.

I pleaded with them to talk with me about their relationship with money and the habits that kept them in this cycle of debt and stress. I told them they needed to set money aside for the future. They refused to have these important conversations. On and on this went for years. Paul stopped working when he was eligible for Social Security. Sharon began telling me that there wasn't enough money for them to continue to live their lifestyle, and she was working more than ever to keep them afloat. For the next ten years, they continued to spend beyond their income, but there were no longer bonuses to rescue them from the debt now.

When Sharon stopped working, I began to notice that her memory was failing. Paul was not in good health at this time either, so I asked them if there was a family member who could help. They didn't want anyone to know about their difficulties and refused to give me a contact. I persisted as I began to see that they were not paying their monthly bills. They finally connected me with Paul's son. When I spoke to him, he was shocked to find out that they had no savings and mounting debt. "My dad always spent like he had plenty of money," he said. I wish that I could tell you that this is an extreme case, but many people find themselves in this circumstance. Paul and Sharon could have made changes that resulted in enjoying their lives *and* taking care of their future. Their refusal to plan led to difficulties for them and for their family.

The *beginner pitfall* can be avoided by putting yourself on high alert about the way you react to new situations. At this point in my life, I have confidence about most things I do, and I masterfully avoid everything else! Whenever I do something new, I have to confront my inner five-year-old, who was terrified to go to kindergarten. New experiences bring up feelings of anxiety for me. Knowing this about myself is very helpful. Think about the reaction you have when starting something new. Whether it is a new job, a new gym, or travel to somewhere you have never been, there is a way of being that emerges. Being aware of that and noticing it as you work on your relationship with money will help you to separate the two experiences. Whenever we learn something new, we manage the new information and skills and simultaneously manage the feelings of being a beginner. Make sure to pay attention to this so that you don't mistake the beginner reaction for any challenges you encounter in learning.

If you are in a relationship, beware of the *couples pitfall.* You each have a relationship with money. You each have opinions about each other's relationship with money. And you each have ideas about the way money is used for joint and separate choices. If there is a disparity in income, you may brush up against feelings related to independence that are uncomfortable to discuss. Your communication is vital to the success of not just your dreams for the future but also whether you will reach that future together.

Begin by understanding each other's stories. Listen to how your partner describes their period of *discovery* and don't add your opinions to it. Ask questions and share observations that they can consider. Then listen some more. You will serve your relationship best if you can learn your partner's point of view. Once you understand each other's experiences, consider what chapter you each are in at the present time. Remember that you are each writing a story. Don't try to tell one story from this point forward. There is no access to *independence* as a pair! By understanding each other's story, you can overlap as you help each other move forward. You can address the systems in place for managing money in your relationship and determine if they work or need adjustments. When a relationship ends, the unraveling of financial matters is typically filled with the worst of emotions. Your attention on this now will remove one of the greatest pressures that couples face. If money isn't a problem, your relationship is far more likely to be part of your picture of success.

As you determine the chapter you are in at this time, don't be precious about getting it right. Be curious and allow yourself space to understand this new way of thinking. Notice any judgments that arise and let them go quickly. You did exactly what you knew how to do based on your origin story and an education that left money out of the conversation. You were taught 123s and ABCs, but until now, you didn't have access to DEFGHIJ—*discovery, exploration, freedom, growth, harmony, independence,* and *joy*. You are now awakened to the fact that you are writing your story from today forward. To make choices with *financial insight*, focus your level of awareness on your relationship with money and your vision for the future.

CHAPTER 14

# The Financial Facts

When you plan a trip, you choose a destination, and then you map out the course. Many tools exist for planning, from an old-fashioned map to an app that provides every distance and turn. No matter which tool you choose, it is the destination that drives your choices. Using this same idea, you need to describe where you are going in life by defining what success means to you. That vision will change over time, and you will be able to adjust accordingly, but you need to have goals in mind. To begin, we need to check on your current view.

If you are near a window right now, look outside. Look in every direction and see everything you can from this perspective. Now, imagine going up to the roof and looking at the same view. You would likely see points farther away in many directions. When you look at your finances, you need to shift your focus from close up to the bigger picture and from a narrow vision to a broad spectrum of possibilities.

Thinking in a linear fashion is natural and helpful when you take action steps. However, when you plan for a future that you cannot fully predict, having an agile mind that can see many options will open up opportunities that you would otherwise miss. To both demonstrate this and to train your mind in agility, simply sit in a different seat. How do I know that you are sitting in the same seat?! Because we all sit in the same seat, over and over and over again.

My corner of the couch is well worn, but I routinely sit in other seats just to take in the view of my home from different perspectives. Besides seeing where I need to dust or spotting where that missing pair of glasses landed, I see things that matter even more. The painting that hangs over my spot on the couch isn't visible in that comfy corner. From across the room, I can enjoy it. I can be delighted by this art that is often out of view. Making sure that you are skilled at seeing things from many views will allow you to reach a level of confidence in your decision-making that is not available in any other way.

Up until now, your view of the financial facts may be deep in the details without a big picture. You move through each day, week, and month with the focus on meeting obligations. The story that you used to tell about your financial circumstances was told in sweeping statements. To turn your vision into action steps, you need to engage with your data in a way that gives you the optimal view. If you are bracing yourself for this conversation about data, wanting to run away, or starting to fall asleep, take a breath. Stay with me! We will start by breaking this down into four workable areas: income, accumulation, spending, and debt management. Then, we will make sure you are sitting in some new seats to view these areas in ways you had not considered before.

Income includes all inflows. Your primary source of income is likely from work. If you have a traditional job with a salary, or hourly pay, your income is predictable. You can pay attention to the frequency and plan for routines. If you are a freelancer or artist, this is considered self-employment, which makes you an ifcome® earner.

I'll never forget the first time I used the word ifcome®. I was in a coaching session with Marc, an actor, and we were discussing the fluctuating and uncertain income that artists must manage. He said, "No one seems to understand. I can't plan anything. I don't know how much money I will make in the next six months, never mind in the following year! I just do what I have to do to and, hopefully, pay my bills." Marc shared the common narrative of the "starving artist." This long-held belief suggests that only the rare few, lucky artists are financially successful. For the rest, it will always be a state of struggle. I assured him that ifcome® is not a barrier to success.

Whether you are an artist, such as a performer, writer, or creator of any kind, or a business owner, like a real estate agent, coach, or other entrepreneur, you are an ifcome® earner. Your income may be sporadic, fluctuating, and unpredictable. Because the financial industry focuses on steady income and doesn't strive to understand ifcome® earners, you may often feel like you don't have access to quality information. If you are an ifcome® earner, rest assured that with *financial insight*, we honor the challenges of ifcome®. Using your values and data, you will more easily determine the levels of stability and flexibility you want to maintain. This leads to confidence in your decision-making process because you are able to balance your career choices with all of your values.

No matter how you earn your income, when you look at it from the view of a month, or even a year, it is limiting. Let's sit in a different seat and see how it changes your view. Imagine being given $1,000,000 when you were twenty-two years old, with the condition that this was all you had to work with for the next twenty years. How do you think you would approach making your decisions? You would likely be thoughtful about choosing a place to live and activities that you enjoy. You would think about making those funds last and wonder if you could make it grow. The lump sum allows you to think about this money from a big picture view.

Let's change this view and see how it impacts your thoughts. Receiving payments of $50,000 per year over twenty years is also a total of $1,000,000. Do you notice a shift in your mindset? How do you think you would approach making your decisions with an annual payment rather than a lump sum?

This is a good moment to pause and notice if you are judging that annual amount and deeming yourself as winning or losing. The median income in the United States in 2022, depending on location, approximated $50,000.[11] You earn based on the choices that you made thus far. It is not good or bad. It is part of the story you write. The intent of this comparison is not judgment but instead to look at income with a longer view. This will help you make decisions about your next steps.

I spoke to thirty-year-old Matthew when I helped him to project his income for the next ten years. When he realized that his $70,000 salary would continue to increase each year and he would have the potential to earn more than $750,000 by his fortieth birthday, he was stunned into silence. Even after taxes, more than $350,000 would move through his hands. He would decide how every dollar of that would be used. I asked him to consider a few questions to help determine next steps. How much did he want to save by the end of the ten years? How much did he want to use for his home? Was he interested in pursuing a higher degree to increase his earnings? Was he interested in reducing spending to work less? Did he want to find a partner who earned as much or more? Suddenly, a world of options became available.

There may come a point when you stop earning from work. There are a variety of life circumstances that can lead to this. No matter what the cause, this is why saving for the future is important. When you stop earning, your spending does not cease. You still need a place to live, food, and activities to enjoy living. When we are young, it is difficult to see this part of life clearly. Our autonomy over money is so shiny and new, and we just want to do things and get stuff! Setting money aside for a future that seems so far away is not compelling at that time.

This is why having a vision is crucial. See beyond your work life to what will bring you happiness and imagine how you want to live in each decade of your life. Those ideas become reality when you start to

---

11 Census Bureau Median Family Income by Family Size, January 22, 2023, https://www.justice.gov/ust/eo/bapcpa/20220401/bci_data/median_income_table.htm.

point money at them. This is not about setting an unchangeable path or committing to plans in the distant future. This is about creating the opportunity to make those choices as time passes. Saving for a down payment on a home doesn't mean that you have to buy a home. The process of saving is to create the opportunity to buy a home if you choose to in the future.

I prefer the word *accumulation* to saving. Saving sounds like you push money away, while accumulation feels like you gather it. Accumulating for your future self is different than saving for someday. Setting yourself up for peace of mind, long-term goals, or planning for a specific event is always for you. If your story to date lacks in this area, simply let go of the past and start today.

When you accumulate money, it can be used to produce more income through investing. The income from investments can then be used for your spending. This connection between the financial areas needs to be part of your plan. It is important to reflect on the way you were telling your story to transform your relationship with money. If you used to describe a paycheck-to-paycheck existence, while noting that you wished you could save for the future, there is a disconnect that you cannot continue to overlook. The choices that you make that prevent you from truly taking care of yourself now and later need your attention. Remember that you have to be willing to step through the doorway of *freedom*. Being proactive by making a new choice is an opportunity that you create with your actions. If you bought a home at the top of your available funds, you created a pressure that can be changed with a different choice. By reducing that cost and accumulating, you set yourself up for other things that are important to you.

Dave and Kate started our first conversation by saying, "Our home is nonnegotiable. We love it, and we are not moving."

"Why is that the first thing you shared?" I asked. I thought that was an odd way to kick off the conversation.

"We're struggling to meet the mortgage payment, but we want our children to be in this specific school district," Kate answered. "We both work full time and have second jobs, so it's important to live nearby to avoid a long commute. The neighboring towns don't have good schools, so we have to stay here."

This was a lot to unpack in just the first five minutes. The limiting belief that making it through each month was the best they could do prevented them from even considering a course correction. Education and family were included in the list of values that they each identified, but their family time was limited because of their work schedules. They wanted to travel because they considered that an important part of education and family time. There was no money being planned for that or for college for their children.

Once they realized that they were not seeing the bigger picture, we began to plan action steps. Kate worked in education, so she found a position in a private school where they could enroll their children for free. With the concern about the school district resolved, they found a home that reduced their costs, allowing them to address more of their priorities. They chose to keep Dave's second job to use the income only for vacations. The motivations now informed their choices. After just a few years, Kate chose to add a second job to accelerate their accumulation. They enjoyed fulfilling work, balanced family time, and planned for the years ahead without pressure and inspired by a vision. They were free at any time to let go of the second jobs and make other adjustments. It was a period of *growth* that had them curious and making new decisions as they understood the relationship between their choices today and the outcomes for tomorrow.

With many data points to consider, spending is the most robust area of your finances. Checking your bank balance is not enough to determine if you point money at what matters to you. Looking at the details, sorted by meaningful categories and compared over a period of months, will give you a fresh view of this information. Have you noticed that you are nearing the end of a book about finances and the word *budget* has not been used? I don't talk about budgets because they are useless. Setting rules that you won't follow is a waste of your time and energy.

Instead, review the prior three, six, or twelve months of your spending to identify patterns. Your recent history will reveal so much more than you can begin to imagine. You will find relief in knowing where the money goes. If you see some spending that doesn't feel aligned with your values, that may seem like bad news, but it is actually great news! Being aware of the issue is your opportunity to work on it. Choose just one category, think about why the amount feels off to you, consider the habits, and get to work on changing just that one thing. Practice for a few months. Be curious. When that is resolved, you can choose to work on another category.

The connections between income, accumulation, and spending become clearer as you learn more about each. If you have debt, the focus will be on managing the debt along with your decisions in the other areas. Managing debt is about creating a plan for paying it off, based on a realistic timeline. It is not necessary to prioritize debt over accumulation. As a matter of fact, doing so will likely continue the debt cycle for a much longer period of time than is necessary. The pressure that you feel to pay off debt is in the way, so let's reset your thoughts about debt.

When you buy something without the funds to do so, you incur debt. Debt is simply past spending. All of the negative emotions related to debt are unnecessary and unhelpful. If you have debt, it is a financial fact. Whether it was for a home, an education, a vacation, or groceries, you gained something before you were able to pay for it. Are you grateful for what you gained? If so, why do you feel bad, instead of grateful? When I was in debt, I knew that I had taken some amazing trips, and I wouldn't trade those experiences for anything. I was also able to look at the cost of those trips, including the credit card interest, and learn from that for future decisions. Being upset about the debt doesn't reduce it any faster! Trying to reduce debt faster by delaying accumulation will lead you right back to debt. The best way to end the debt cycle is a combination of paying debt and accumulating. When the debt is paid off, you will have what you simultaneously accumulated to keep you from ever needing to use debt again. Debt management shifts the conversation from paying off debt to eliminating stress now and for the future.

Each of the four financial areas are vital to your success. You may find yourself wanting to focus on some more than others. Notice what feels most comfortable and then make sure to give the proper attention to the other areas too. Your knowledge about each should ultimately be equal. Once you feel comfortable with all four areas, you are best equipped to make them work together.

CHAPTER 15

# Course Correction

My grandmother sometimes reminded me, "Into each life some rain must fall." I assumed it was the wisdom of old age until I looked up the origin. Henry Wadsworth Longfellow was thirty-five years old when he wrote this![12] I can picture him sitting down to tell me his financial situation and starting with this thought. It is a poet's version of what I hear over and over again. You will not escape life without some obstacles, and some of the challenges you face will be the direct result of a choice you made.

Every choice will result in a new circumstance. That circumstance may be the desired outcome, something that approximates the desired outcome, or an undesired outcome also known as a consequence. For most of us, we learn this lesson very young. In elementary school, we experience consequences in many ways. We see how our choices impact our friendships and how studying impacts our scores on tests. We test limits by behaving well to receive rewards and by misbehaving to find our boundaries. The connection between our choice and the result is often clear and direct. It isn't until we have autonomy, particularly over money, that this becomes more complicated. When the choices you make are more significant, the result takes longer to reveal itself.

---

12 Khurana, Simran, "Poet Henry Wadsworth Longfellow," ThoughtCo, August 26, 2020, thoughtco.com/the-rainy-day-quotes-2831517.

Through the lens of *financial insight,* you can connect the dots with ease and confidence.

Beth had worked in fundraising since she graduated from college. She always had strong feelings about having an impact and expected her work in not-for-profit organizations would be fulfilling. Her first job was not satisfying, and she believed the working environment wasn't quite right for her. She moved on to a different organization and found that she was still not finding any satisfaction in the work.

She was approached by a recruiter and offered another job with significantly higher pay and chose to take that opportunity. She hoped that if she was better compensated, she would like her work more. While she worked in this job, an unexpected development occurred in another area of her life. While they had previously discussed their uncertainty about having a family, her husband, Kevin, now expressed a real desire to be a father. Feeling that she had not yet found her place in her career, adding the possible role of mother made this a confusing time. After many conversations and a lot of careful thought, she agreed to start their family with the understanding that she and her husband would share equally in all responsibilities for their child.

Even though she had not yet found inspiration in her work, having a fulfilling career was a priority for her. When her son was born, she and Kevin each had family leave that allowed them to coordinate their time off to care for the newborn. They planned to start childcare after his first birthday. They spent a lot of time discussing how they felt about taking time off and how much fulfilling work meant to each of them. Beth continued to wonder why she couldn't connect to the work she was doing. Her son was two years old when she was wandering around the library with him. She watched him interacting with books and started to notice a librarian working with a group of students.

Suddenly, there was a thought that she never considered before. This place felt like home to her. She loved being surrounded by books. She couldn't help but wonder what it would be like to be a librarian.

She couldn't get this thought out of her mind, and when she shared it with Kevin, he said, "Do it!" His reaction shocked her. She didn't have the qualifications and would need to obtain another degree to pursue this. They had started a family and needed both of their salaries to accomplish their goals for home ownership, as well as many other future plans. Was she supposed to work, be a mother, and go to school? Kevin, ever the supporter, simply said, "Yes, let's figure it out."

There had been many significant life choices before Beth discovered what she really wanted to do in her career. She went to a great school, married, moved to a new city, worked in three organizations, and had a child. When she realized that happiness was outside of her grasp until she made a change in her career, she had to navigate a course correction that would impact every part of her life.

When you find yourself in circumstances that are not optimal, recognizing that a course correction is needed may be challenging. Because you have invested time, energy, and money in a choice, the thought of unwinding it can be daunting. It is natural to initially avoid the change. A course correction may appear to take you out of your comfort zone, but the opposite is true. By staying in a situation that isn't working, you are already in a discomfort zone. Some of the biggest challenges, like a change in career or ending a relationship, don't happen because you are comfortable! Yet you perceive the course correction as causing discomfort. If you avoid the course correction, you make a choice that could cause you to live unhappily ever after.

*Growth*, inevitably, requires some course correction. If this strikes you as bad news, pause and think it through. It's great news! When you reach this chapter, you want to consider all options. This is the most empowering time in your life. You have enough knowledge about yourself to clarify a vision for the future. You have the power to make changes. You have many years ahead to reap the benefits of the changes you make. The adjustments that you consider may be significant, or they may be subtle. Remember, these are options, and you don't have to change anything. But if you are aware that your path is not leading you to your vision, choosing a course correction is for your benefit. This is not intended to be disruptive. In fact, it is more likely that the course correction will rectify a previous disruption on your path to your best life.

Beth considered leaving work and going to school full time. She and Kevin could use what they accumulated for a down payment to supplement his salary if they delayed their goal of home ownership by at least a few years. While she wanted to leave her current job as soon as possible, she also wanted them to be settled in a home when their son began school. These competing goals brought everything into question. She found a program she could attend part-time, but that meant staying in her current job longer. After careful thought, she chose to take this longer path. The option to deplete savings to achieve the career change did not align with the other priorities in their lives. The process that Beth and Kevin went through to make this decision was thoughtful. They asked bidirectional questions, like, "How will home ownership impact our careers?" and "How will our careers impact home ownership?" They weighed the impact of using student loans or using savings to pay for this education. They considered Beth's age when she would start her new career and the age of their son when they settled into a new home.

Course correction, when done in a thoughtful way, is extraordinary. I see this time and time again when an individual's choices align with their truest desire. The desired outcome is enhanced by unexpected opportunities. About a year into Beth's part-time pursuit of the new degree, Kevin received a job offer. His salary would grow significantly, and the job was in an area where they were excited to buy a home. Beth could leave her job and complete her education in a much shorter period than they planned. It is not unusual for a little magic to show up when you are on the right path!

In Beth and Kevin's circumstances, there was a lot of opportunity to make a thoughtful course correction. That isn't the case for everyone. If you are aware of a course correction that you desire but cannot see the path to make that happen, it will seem dark and dreary, like Longfellow's Rainy Day. You might feel trapped in the consequences of earlier decisions. Recognizing the desire for the course correction may not be an exciting revelation at first, but the alternative of not opening yourself up to the possibility will leave you stuck. This is the sad circumstance that many people grapple with because they have not created opportunities by managing their finances in a way that gives them the flexibility to make a change. Even so, this is not the end of the road.

Remember that *growth* comes after *freedom*. Whether consequences of prior choices are the catalyst, or you are being proactive, *freedom* is an opportunity that you choose. Your decision process becomes more and more refined as you learn to align your vision for the future with your values and your data. When you recognize that a course correction will move you in the direction of your best life, you make a series of decisions. The first is the decision to work on the change. If you are not ready to embrace the change and do it thoughtfully, slow down. Making an abrupt change may lead you to another difficult circumstance. Once you achieve clarity that a course correction is desirable, plan it and move forward, allowing yourself time to do it well. Begin with the easiest changes first and only work on one at a time.

The timeline for the change will be determined by the choices you make from today forward. When I realized that I wanted to move, I didn't do this all on day one. If I chose to make a sudden move, I would have ended up in an apartment or neighborhood that wouldn't have achieved the desired outcome. Instead, I thought about my spending and worked on the habits to allow me to focus on paying off debt. I began looking at the cost of apartments in different neighborhoods to help determine how much I needed to spend each month after I moved. I decided how much I wanted to have in savings before I made this move. By taking my time to pay off the debt and achieve a level of stability, I was able to make the move in a way that brought me to the *joy* that I was seeking.

The desired outcome informs the course correction, and the quality of course correction determines the success of the desired outcome. By focusing on the vision, leveraging time, clarifying your values, and understanding your data, you write the next chapter of your story with a level of intent that you could not have had before this moment.

CHAPTER 16

# Writing with Intention

You now possess the awareness needed to be the author of the life story you want to tell. You know that with each decision you make, you write your story. Your understanding of the chapters—*discovery, exploration, freedom, growth, harmony, independence,* and *joy*—relieves the previous pressure and allows you to confidently take the steps to move in the direction of your best life. You have been writing the story all along, but now, you write with intention.

Enjoy defining where you want to go on this journey. Start with a dream and be curious. Aim to strike a balance between learning about your relationship with money and beginning to take action steps with *financial insight*. Keeping in mind that every choice you make writes your story, starting to be thoughtful about your choices today is a positive step. Noticing habits that might hinder you is an act of mindfulness. When you work in this way, you will be amazed by the feelings and thoughts that come to you. Avoid getting stuck in financial paralysis by making decisions and taking action to move in a direction that you believe will make you happy. If the direction is not right, welcome this news and course correct promptly. Even the wrong path is great information when you are thoughtful.

Embrace being a beginner while learning how to align your values and data. I have to say it one last time to make sure it sticks: *no two people with the same amount of money make the same choices*. You are the one and only, true and original, you. It is your happily ever after that determines each decision made along the path. Professionals can guide you in the best use of your resources only if you paint the picture.

Create an environment that supports you when you are in action. Systems that help you understand the financial facts don't have to be fancy. Focus on meaningful information, managed easily and consistently. Set the parameters for checking in on your progress, including measures of success, like feeling ease, stability, confidence, and freedom in your plan. Connect the dots from your previous mindset to your new understanding to avoid backsliding. Skip any comparisons to other people or their lives. The only measure that can truly guide you is where you are today compared to where you want to be.

I have witnessed lives improve over and over. The shift becomes natural. Whenever someone starts their journey, I am reminded of Jennifer, one of the first students in FIT. At our initial meeting, she was afraid to say that she dreamed of travel. She thought saying this out loud would lead to shame because she didn't believe she could ever afford to make this a part of her life. She went on her dream trip to Japan a year later, the first of three extraordinary trips over the next five years.

For each part of your story, make your goals real, not fairy tales, by stating them with a timeline. When you are specific about a date, you change the way you approach the goal. Declaring "I'm going to buy a home someday" is not enough. What action steps will you take based on this declaration? You will likely talk about it. You might even set some money aside. When you scroll through real estate apps and see homes that seem out of reach, you might give up. You might talk about this for a decade with no action taken. Instead, choose a date and declare it. If you say, "I'm going to buy a home in five years," what is your first action step? You will look for homes in areas that interest you. You will determine cost and calculate a down payment. You will divide that amount over five years and determine if it is possible to accumulate that amount. The date is not intended as a deadline but instead is a *working when* to help you plan. You might adjust the timeline if you feel you need more time or if you can achieve your goal more quickly. Or you may notice that you are not committed to this dream, and you can move on to another one that truly inspires you.

A *working when* is far more empowering than someday or a deadline. Your success is determined by your process and progress. Declaring a date and then using that date in your planning will guide you to find your path. A deadline creates pressure in a pass/fail, win/lose mentality. By establishing a *working when*, you create space to learn. I gave myself seven years to move from New Jersey to New York City because I thought it would take me that long to pay off my debt and accumulate enough to feel comfortable with the increase in expenses. I accomplished that goal in two years because once I had the vision, the choices became easier. I began to see how each financial area impacted the others. I worked on the plan consistently and found that I could do much more than I anticipated. Had I set the *working when* at two years and found that it was too much pressure, I could have extended the time. Having the *working when* establishes an environment for success. You will either thrive in the plan or adjust it, but you will do so from a place of clarity.

When the goal is for a longer term, you also want to create benchmarks by which to measure your progress. If you are thirty-five years old and you want to stop working and travel at age fifty-five, you have twenty years of action steps ahead. We start with projecting the cost to travel in the way you dream of in twenty years. Where will you live? What will you need to be happy? Answers to these questions inform the plan for accumulation between now and then. You determine how much is available now and what you can accumulate routinely. Are there bonuses or other resources to consider? Are there adjustments in your spending that you want to test? Will it mean downsizing your home at some point? Designating check-ins, at least annually for a goal of this magnitude, is important. You want to determine what works or does not work so you can make adjustments. You may find that you are doing more than anticipated or less. The benchmarks along the way may be increases in your income, the amount accumulated, and the end of some types of spending. When a debt is paid off, like a student loan, does that monthly payment add to the accumulation for this long-term plan?

It is never too soon to begin planning, and it is never too late, unless you don't start today! Now is the right time. It is in this moment that you decide on your future. And now again in this moment, and now, again, in this moment. Forget the idea of your next birthday or New Year's Day. Every choice you make today determines your next chapter. Listen to your future self, of five, ten, twenty years from now, and more. In the same way that you wish you could tell your younger self some of the lessons you learned, a future you would like your attention today.

APPENDIX A

# Financial Insight Chapter Guide

Begin the work of *financial insight* by understanding where you are in your story. Start with *discovery* and work your way forward. As you move through the questions for each chapter, you will come upon some that feel very current. This will help you determine what phase you are in at this time.

You can also come back to this guide as you take your next steps. It will serve as a resource to keep you moving from chapter to chapter. The cyclical nature of our lives will have you moving from *joy* back to *discovery* over the years. As your skills of *financial insight* strengthen over time, you will likely find that *exploration, freedom,* and *growth* start to blend into a much shorter process. Each new level of *joy* builds on the next, and you will write your story with ease and confidence.

***Discovery* Questions:**

*Awareness* begins with your earliest money memory.

- How old were you at the time of this memory?
- How did you perceive and interpret this experience as a child?
- Stepping back into your adult mind, how do you describe this event?

- If you weren't the child in the memory, would you tell the story differently?
- How does this show up in your current relationship with money?

*Attention* begins with your earliest memory of making choices with money.

- Describe the kinds of choices you made. Did you spend without thinking? Were you extra cautious?
- Did you seek guidance or approval? How did you aim to be more independent in your choices?
- How were the influential people in your life supportive or critical of your approach?
- What are your most vivid memories in this period? Repeat the questions related to awareness for this memory to see how it impacts you now.

*Autonomy* begins when you earn money.

- What do you remember about your first paycheck? Did you have your own bank account? How did the adults in your life guide your steps?
- What age do you remember a feeling of being on your own? Did this feel like a sudden change? Did you feel prepared?
- What feelings about autonomy carried through to your relationship with money today?

***Exploration* Questions:**

- How have you allowed yourself time to understand who you are as an adult? Do you need more time in this inquiry?
- What voice do you hear most clearly? Is it yours, or are you often influenced by others?
- What thoughts arise for you based on your age, experience, and where you think you *should* be?
- What decisions do you recall that led you to positive outcomes?

- What decisions do you recall that didn't work out? What lessons can you take from these circumstances?

***Freedom* Questions:**

- How would you describe your willingness to make changes that would lead to stability and happiness in your life?
- How prepared do you feel to make decisions when opportunities are presented to you or when unexpected circumstances alter your existing plans?
- What questions do you have about what you want or how to obtain what you want?

***Growth* Questions:**

- What areas of your life have you considering a course correction?
- What are the current steps you are taking or hope to take?
- What do you need to learn now to plan your next action steps?

***Harmony* and *Independence* Questions:**

- Which present commitments seem to prevent you from even dreaming about changes that would make you happier in your life?
- How much time do you need to create the stability for a significant change?
- How would a change in career, home, or family impact you or others who rely on you?

***Joy* Questions:**

- What is your definition of success?
- Which areas of your life currently provide you with feelings of happiness and satisfaction?
- Having achieved success, what are you curious about for your future?

APPENDIX B

# About FIT

Congratulations on taking the first step on your *financial insight* journey. I invite you to continue in the FIT Universe, a place where money is not just approachable but also the focus as a foundational component of happiness. Understanding now that you are already writing your story with every decision you make, it is time to transform from passively writing to writing with intention.

In the FIT Universe, you will learn the principles of *financial insight*, clarify your values, understand your data, and receive personal guidance to transform your new awareness into action.

The FIT Universe, conveniently accessible online via desktop or mobile app, includes everything you need to support you:

> **The Courses** – Fundamentals, Insight, Ifcome®, and Benchmark are the four courses in the FIT curriculum. These courses comprise recorded video lessons that average just eight minutes each. Money happens in real time in our lives, so the habit of consistency in our attention to it is built into the curriculum. No one is too busy for these programs.
>
> **The Coaching** – Private coaching with me is included for every member in the FIT Universe. It is my top priority to make sure we spend time together to discuss your

circumstances. These sessions provide personalized support to help you implement all that you learn.

**The Community** – Live, virtual workshops enhance the learning in the courses. The group dynamic in these conversations is beneficial to all participants. As you recognize that we all have similar feelings, regardless of our circumstances, you gain more confidence. This is also additional time for Q&A with me on special topics like ifcome®, home buying, managing finances as a couple, and so much more.

After years, and perhaps decades, of navigating money on your own, it will take some effort to transform the habits and behaviors that you have practiced for so long. Join me in the FIT Universe to be fully supported while learning about your relationship with money, defining what success means to you, and writing the next chapter in your story with *financial insight*.

APPENDIX C

# Values Exercise

Knowing what matters most to you sounds like it should be easy to identify. Unfortunately, we are bombarded with so many messages about priorities that we get confused. The *shoulds* take over, and we lose our most basic understanding of self.

To help you launch your FIT Journey, I invite you join me for the *Values Exercise*. In this video, I will guide you through the exercise and give you the best practices for making your values intuitive.

https://financialinsighttraining.com/values-exercise/

Made in the USA
Middletown, DE
07 November 2023